AF449767

THE
QUEEN
WITHIN

THE QUEEN WITHIN

10 Principles of the Authentic
Feminine Power & Sensuality

JUSTINA CARMO

The Queen Within
@2019, Justina Carmo

Self-editing and design: Justina Carmo
First edition: November 2019

ISBN: 978-84-18098-47-5

*To my beloved sister, Dominika.
May this book be the guide on your path
To expressing your femininity as a Queen that you are.
I love you.*

WHAT'S NEXT?

1. Discover the full "Rich Soul" trilogy

Click in: www.justinacarmo.com

#2 STEP — Blend Your Spirituality With Your Financial Success

You've been repeating "I can't afford" for way too long. It's time to reclaim your abundant destiny with money.

In this book, I will guide you on how to express your ambition to attract success while taking full control of your mind, your emotions and your checking account.

#3 STEP — Turn Your Gifts Into Gold & Let Your Superpowers Shine!

Deep inside, you're hiding a best-selling author. An international motivational speaker. A multimillionaire girl boss. A highly successful investor. A dream woman. And you know it.

In *Spiritual Superstar"* not only will you be given the necessary knowledge to empower yourself from within but also you will be given resources and exercises to make measurable changes in becoming visible and fully expressed in your biggest gift. No more shrinking. No more hiding. No more holding back.

WHO'S JUSTINA CARMO?

Hello Sunshine,

This is a super short and sweet sheet welcoming you into my world.

I'm Justina and I help spiritual women like you reconnect with their femininity and heal their finances.

At the moment I live in Barcelona, Spain. Have you ever been? I'm in love with the country so much I'm planning to stay permanently.

I use my Lululemon pants for rainy day hangs instead of actually working out, but when the sun's out you'll see me with my Dior lipstick on and smiling.

I'm Eastern European, Polish to be precise — which means I have a tendency to tell it like it is, but it works beautifully in my coaching business because we bulldoze through barriers quick smart.

There's no way I could ever overdose on reggaeton music and have been known to play one song 6 times in a row. I know you can too, because Despacito.

I'm a material girl and a lover of all things luxe and posh, but I'm also a spiritual girl. It's true, sometimes the best things in life are free. Like morning barefoot walks on the beach.

I've been through my own magical transformation, in my business and in my life, and I can't wait to share my journey with you as we hang out in the following pages....

I'd love to know this before we start…

YOU'RE ONLY ONE DECISION AWAY FROM YOUR GREATEST DESTINY....

ODE TO A "TOO MUCH" WOMAN

There she is. The "too much" woman. The one who loves too hard, feels too deeply, asks too often, desires too much.

There she is taking up too much space, with her laughter, her curves, her honesty, her sexuality. Her presence is as tall as a tree, as wide as a mountain. Her energy occupies every crevice of the room. Too much space she takes.

There she is causing a ruckus with her persistent wanting, too much wanting. She desires a lot, wants everything—too much happiness, too much alone time, too much pleasure. She'll go through brimstone, murky river, and hellfire to get it. She'll risk all to quell the longings of her heart and body. This makes her dangerous.

She is dangerous.

And there she goes, that "too much" woman, making people think too much, feel too much, swoon too much. She with her authentic prose and self-assuredness in the way she carries herself. She with her belly laughs and her insatiable appetite and her proneness to fiery passion. All eyes on her, thinking she's hot shit.

Oh, that "too much" woman. . . too loud, too vibrant, too honest, too emotional, too smart, too intense, too pretty, too difficult, too sensitive, too wild, too intimidating, too success-ful, too fat, too strong, too political, too joyous, too needy—too much.

She should simmer down a bit, be taken down a couple of notches. Someone should put her back in a more respectable place. Someone should tell her.

Here I am, the Too Much Woman, with my too-tender heart and my too-much emotions.

I want a lot — justice, sincerity, spaciousness, ease, intimacy, actualisation, respect, to be seen, to be understood, your undivided attention, and all of your promises to be kept.

I've been called high maintenance because I want what I want and intimidating because of the space I occupy. I've been called selfish because I am self-loving. I've been called a witch because I know how to heal myself.

And still. I rise. Still, I want and feel and ask and risk and take up space.

I must.

Us Too Much Women have been facing extermination for centuries—we are so afraid of her, terrified of her big presence, of the way she commands respect and wields the truth of her feelings. We've been trying to stifle the Too Much Woman for ions—in our sisters, in our wives, in our daughters. And even now, even today, we shame the Too Much Woman for her bigness, for her wanting, for her passionate nature.
And still, she thrives.

In my own world and before my very eyes, I am witnessing the reclamation and rising up of the Too Much Woman. That Too Much Woman is also known to some as Wild Woman or the Divine Feminine. In any case, she is me, she is you, and she is loving that she's finally, finally getting some airtime.

If you've ever been called "too much," or "overly emotional," or "bitchy," or "stuck up," you are likely a Too Much Woman.

And if you are. . . I implore you to embrace all that you are—all of your depth, all of your vastness; to not hold yourself in, and to never abandon yourself, your bigness, your radiance.

Forget everything you've heard—your too much-ness is a gift; oh yes, one that can heal, incite, liberate, and cut straight to the heart of things.

Do not be afraid of this gift, and let no one shy you away from it. Your too much-ness is magic, is medicine. It can change the world.

Don't believe me? Check this: All of your favorite women, the ones who've made history, the ones who've lent their voices for change and have courageously given themselves permission to be exactly who they are. Some examples: Oprah, Ronda Rousey, Beyoncé, Kali, Misty Copeland, Janet Mock, Mary Magdalene . . . they're all Too Much Women.

So please, Too Much Woman: Ask. Seek. Desire. Expand. Move. Feel. Be.

Make your waves, fan your flames, give us chills.

Please, rise.

We need you.

By Ev'Yan Whitney

CONTENTS

INTRODUCTION

For Such A Time As This, You've Been Called To Be
The Queen

When I think about all the books on female empowerment, I realise that many of us seek all the answers outside of ourselves: ask your mentor, get slimmer, colour your hair, change the way you dress, move to a different place or career…But I have found them to always be a secondary piece of a required bigger shift - a fundamental change of who we are as feminine women, living in times of unprecedented access to technology, career possibilities and freedom of expression.

As an experienced coach, author and intuitive healer who supports women's souls daily, I have been privileged to witness some of the most beautiful transformations in the lives of individuals and their families when overcoming their insecurities, own their worth and see themselves as peaceful, divine and noble. Women who claim their own sense of self-worth and purpose in the world.

It's time for a new period in your life. The one giving yourself permission to shine and be your uninhibited self. To become The Woman you want to be. The woman who has it all: the healthy body, the supportive relationship, her trusted circle and is relaxed around her finances because she is supported in her higher purpose.

You may be going through a period in your life where Queen is the last thing you feel like. You'd rather say you that you're a neglected Cinderella. The unappreciated little match girl, desperately trying to make ends meet in any way possible, or the unmothered ugly duckling, yearning to belong and finally feel safe and protected.

We've all been there. We've all been through those dark moments when we didn't believe our potential to ascend to the position of a Queen.

Who, me?! Me, as the Queen? HELLO Justina?! Just look at me. Look at my tired face, neglected hair, old clothes and shoes. I feel alone and I'm tired of constantly struggling. I don't even look like a Queen, rather like a beggar or a servant. It's hard to believe I could become one if my life is in such a mess.

I hear you. Breathe. Relax. Calm down your judging mind.

No matter how much your core is shaken, your essence remains unchanged. God has been preparing you for your greatest destiny. His ways are not our ways, yet we must trust them. This book is your training and elevation to a new state of being in the world. You called it in. Wanted it. So receive it.

Just like a lotus flower grows out of the mud, Queens are elevated from an unfavourable environment; unsupportive relationships that seemed too limiting for a Queen-to-become or life difficulties that ultimately polished her character into excellence and compassion. God hasn't chosen you just for your virtues but also for your faults. In God's eyes you are perfect for the mission you've been chosen for.

On your quest for your own Queenhood, the answers lie within, deep in your heart. The solutions lie in the integration of your light self and your shadow self. In the integration of your empowered feminine side and your empowered masculine side.

The Queen within is your higher self. The highest expression of you. Your soul. She's been limited, forgotten and repressed. Yet, if you picked up this book and you're holding it in your hands, I'll say it to you again, despite your initial disbelief: *You've been chosen to become the Queen. To save your people. To be the healing voice and presence in the hearts of men and women who will come into contact with you.*

Your Queen consciousness and state of being requirements continuous empowerment, attention and your willingness to listen to it. I present myself here as your dignified, yet humble soul sister, helping you to mend those parts, your life and consciousness, that were broken as a result of repressing your Queen within.

My intention for this book is that you accept your calling to become aware of the Queen that God has created for you. My desire is that after reading this book, you will be a Queen about challenging situations in your life which previously you avoided or withdrew from. That you will reclaim your inner power to access your strong, unstoppable and unapologetic self.

I will guide you through a self-empowering journey towards your Queenhood. If some ideas seem repetitive, they are there to remind you about something I want you to pay special attention to. As you will see, the repetition of actions and behaviours is key to your success and transformation. From my experience of working with private clients and hosting training, seminars, and webinars, the true knowing happens when we feel the information at the level of your belly, not just conceptually. I desire that the teaching I'm about to share will renovate not only your mind and thoughts, but also your body.

Lastly, one of the key principles of being a Queen is that they are empowered from within. They run on their spiritual energy, self-belief and inner strength gained along their journey. As you move on to applying this teaching and exercises, please don't expect other people around you to "get it" or what you're up to (maybe apart from your other Queen girlfriends).

Some parts of the journey are made alone, in silence and isolation. I will remind you of that many times throughout this book to calm your soul. The reason for this is that whatever prevents you from hearing your Queen and God's voice in your life will have to go…people, places and thoughts. From that clear space, you will also need to take the time to love yourself deeply. Slowly, inch by inch and step by step, we will work on opening your heart wide for love and your gracious disposition to be of service in the world. Your intuition will sharpen. You will dare to be seen as the glorious woman that you are, and speak up for your soul's truth, lovingly and respectfully.

I hope you're as excited about it as I am for you!

HERE'S WHAT YOU CAN EXPECT FROM THIS BOOK:

'd like to present to you what we need to amend, face and tweak together, in order to elevate you to a Queenly status, so that you have total clarity about the process and trust in the journey.

PART I Elevating your Consciousness to the Mindset of a Queen

The transformation will start with an overview of key Queenly principles that you must master to fully maximise your potential as the divine woman that you are. First of all, we will analyse and estimate together where exactly are you in your soul journey. We will take a closer look at what patterns show up in your life and what needs eliminating, upgrading or transforming.

In **Chapter 1 — Queens are empowered from within**, you will be introduced to the mentality of a Queen, and how to start thinking like one. I start here as we are changed by the renovation of our minds. It is important that you begin taking control over the way you think about yourself, the way you react to circumstances and your attitude towards your goals, ambitions, and obligations.

I will guide you through releasing the old paradigm of you as a slave-girl, upgrading to a high-level maid and stepping into the status of a Queen. I've prepared a guided meditation - a set of #crownadjustment exercises you will love, and practical tips that will show you how to implement these practices right away in your daily life. It will be an easy read, I promise.

In **Chapters 2** and **3**, we will look at what it means to *"be a Queen about it"* - to empower yourself to take actions that raise your standards, results, and admiration.

You've probably already heard of the concept that what you focus on expands. But in **Chapter 3, Step 1: A Queen knows only one direction: FORWARD,** I discuss how, if you allow yourself to be stuck by external limitations and avoid being above them, you deny yourself your Queenhood. The result is inertia, insecurities, and helplessness. So in order to empower the Queen Within, you must be bold, brave - go beyond your past pain, struggle and resentment. In this process, you must also stay faithful to your true desires, having the utmost compassion for yourself and your role in the world. Be unapologetic about why and what you desire. In other words, in order to thrive, you must we willing to let your Non- Queen die and allow your real Queen within to take the reins.

Chapter 4: Queens position themselves for greatness, continues to look at how we unconsciously show up as less than Queens and play 'small' out of fearful parts of our personality, in order to please and accommodate our environment. That's why it's not enough to just desire a change but actually commit to it, on a daily basis, in the way we express ourselves, communicate our ideas and even look people in the eyes. By the end of this book, you will know how to present yourself and your body of work with dignity and sincere confidence, without arrogance. After all, us Queens, we keep it classy.

Chapter 5: Queens control their emotions, illustrates the distinction between being manipulated and having self-control.

Being manipulated entails living in ever-lasting emotional drama and functioning as a victim of your circumstances or menstrual cycle, while others have great fun pushing all your buttons and playing you like a fool. Luckily, that game is OVER. Us Queens, we know how to keep it cool. Your emotions are here to guide you, not ruin your life or your finances. We need to shed light on how to take control of our emotions, while at the same time having access and contact with them.

As a result of reading this chapter, you'll become grounded in your body, focused and free from overreacting in a way that harms your relationships or your current reality.

PART II Stepping Towards Your New Destiny as a Queen

In Chapter 6: Queens exude regal presence, you will be shown how to embrace the concept of being the Queen and embodying her right away. Even better, you will know exactly how to connect with your royal presence and show up as Queens do. Yes, that needs training but that's why we'll do it together. I've got your back. I will point out the most common mistakes to avoid and best practices to implement. In that queenly state of being, you will begin to emanate your regal presence during any meeting, date or professional appointment. Thus, if you can mentally and spiritually anchor into your regal presence of the Queen, you will experience the state of being one and what is more, being seen as one.

Now you are moving to your new identity because your mind and body are working as one. When you begin to feel like your presence is sacred, needed and honoured you empower yourself to take more space and influence in your surroundings. You are changing the old subconscious programming that made you think less of yourself and behave as though you didn't matter. These old habits, attitudes, ways of being, go directly to the bin in chapter 6! Adiós, no longer needed! A Queen doesn't waste her energy on trashy thoughts, situations, and behaviours.

Chapter 7: Queens respectfully claim their worth, explores how to break free from the draining habit of undervaluing our gifts and talents, just to be liked and accepted.

A Queen expands her comfort zone by growing steadily. We all reach a certain point when we fear being judged as greedy, materialistic or "all about money". A Queen gives herself permission to fully own the worth of her contribution and has reverence for what she does. Even though she is priceless, she decided that her time and expertise also have their own value. This is the point where your new empowered mindset either takes flight or collapses into repetitive self-deprivation and self-doubt. You will learn to balance your energy by being aligned with purest intentions and grounded reasoning. Ultimately, you will create an undeniable sense of self-worth. When how you appear is who you are, you are truly free.

Part II concludes with **Chapter 8: Queen's dress to project power,** in which my purpose is to demystify the physical appearance of the Queen, so that you know what external image you are choosing for yourself and why.

Discussing fashion style (made simple), I will show you how your looks enhance your reputation when you are dressing with thought and purporse. If nothing in your wardrobe changes and you pay no mindful attention as to how you present yourself to the world, then your journey is not complete. When you are deliberate and intentional with the way you dress, you empower yourself to be seen as the Queen that you are. Truth be told, even Queens in distress do not tolerate yoga pants for too long. What excites us the sensation of being our most beautiful self and what we can create from that level of self-care. Now you will begin to master the art of shining like a diamond.We will cover the core principles of the art of power dressing, so that the golden gates that used to be closed, will open in front of you.

PART III Living Your Life According to Queen's Rules: All of the information in parts I and II are provided in order to equip you with the necessary resources to become a benevolent Queen, who rules with her heart and serves the world greatly. Part III is all about final disposition and performing your God-given assignments. **In Chapter 9: Queens have a powerful relationship with God,** you will be empowered on how to strengthen your relationship with God so that you feel secure from within that you will receive guidance from and remain connected with your creator.

Chapter 10: Queens surrender to Kings. Here, we will discuss the core principles of the Power Couple and your potential alliance with an empowered soul mate, so that you can create a sacred relationship. Even though I will use words like surrendering and being obedient I beg you to stay with me and not pull the pin at this stage! You may be asking yourself, *"Why do I need to surrender to a King or be obedient? No way. Not for me. Thanks!"*

I know. I'd probably be thinking the same. I decided to add this relevant knowledge given the big misunderstanding nowadays of the empowered feminine and masculine and the outcomes we observe: increased divorce rate, couples separating quickly and more and more independent women being frustrated and alone back at home with just some cats, cookies and wine. When you comprehend the what and why, the more you will *know* and *feel* and thus, be in a position to make better-informed choices. I want you to have the power and self-awareness to be confident in surrendering to the guidance that a new, enlightened and emboldened soul will provide your love life.

Let's get started.

PART I

PART I

THE MINDSET OF A QUEEN

Chapter One

QUEENS ARE EMPOWERED FROM WITHIN

"Being powerful is like being a lady.
If you have to tell people you are one, you aren't."
— MARGARET THATCHER

Being a Queen is like being a lady. You won't need to self-proclaim yourself as one. You won't need to announce your arrival. Once you connect with her and embody her in your life, it will show. It will be obvious. Others around you will feel *"Here comes the Queen"*. They will secretly wonder *"What makes her so"* and make space for you to walk by and grace them with your radiant presence.

It's my purpose to raise your consciousness as a woman to that place. It doesn't matter where you're from, how much hardship you've had to endure, or how broken you feel at the moment. What does matter is the divine truth about you, the truth you must remember at all times along this journey:

GOD HAS CREATED YOU TO BE THE QUEEN.

Every woman is destined to be the Queen. Yet, not every woman is open to it. Without consciousness, we can be in front of the very thing we're looking for and not notice. It's similar to a popular story of a beggar who has a £1,000,000 check hidden in his bag without realising it. Does that automatically make him rich? No, not until the moment he becomes aware of what he possesses.

In our modern times, we can observe the rise of the divine feminine consciousness on the planet, its ultimate compassion, intuition, and pure innocence. More and more women across the globe are able to express qualities such as: nurturing, peace-making, forgiving, non-judgmental, intuitive and sensitive.

At the same time, we also see the disrespectful behaviour of women towards themselves and in other women with broken consciousness. By that, I mean inappropriate verbal and physical vulgarity, promiscuity, hostility and acting excessively masculine out of fear.

My intention in this chapter is to explain to you the key principles that compose the mentality of a Queen. I am about to teach you how to start thinking as one and make necessary adjustments as we are transformed by the renovation of our minds. So please approach this book with the clear intention of opening your mind to new ideas and new ways of looking at events in your life

DISCOVER THE QUEEN THAT LIVES WITHIN YOU

Deep within you always knew you've been called to live a big, beautiful life and impact the lives of others in your unique way. Correct me if I'm wrong, but... haven't you always been attracted to stylish clothes, impressive houses, and classy women? Deep within your soul, you heard that little voice telling you that were made for so much more. That voice is your TRUTH. Your pureness. Your way to liberation.

You'll be required to connect with this voice and check in with your intuition on a regular basis. You do it via daily spiritual practices like journalling, prayer meditation and setting clear intentions. What is more, you'll be required to trust it and follow the guidance – even when its purpose is not always clear to you. Hold tight and don't freak out. The good news is God has already prepared the way. He's preparing you now.

SHRINKING BACK IS NO LONGER AVAILABLE. AS SCARY AS IT MAY BE, MOVING FORWARD IS YOUR ONLY OPTION.

Your royal journey to Queenhood — the full expression of you as a divine feminine woman — begins deep within. It starts with permission to be yourself. It begins the moment you've had enough playing at being Cinderella, neglected and hiding your full potential. Your soul always knew better. I bet. You wouldn't have picked up a book about being a Queen otherwise.

Consciousness is the new sexy

Before I introduce you to the concept of the Queen and portray it in more detail, I'd like to set out an intention with you.

Just take a breath in between these lines.

Stop.

Gently place a hand on your heart and think within:

> *"My intention is to have more compassion for myself during my process. I give myself permission to think more kindly, beautifully and lovingly about myself, even when I'm challenged or feel confused."*

Our inner talk creates our outer world. That harsh, nagging voice within you is not your soul's voice. It probably sounds more like your mum or dad that you had internalised…Start becoming more aware of your inner dialogue by catching yourself with an "AHA! moment" — here it comes again — criticising me or scaring me! Change it immediately into *"My beautiful, of <u>course</u> you're able to do it. You can succeed at this!"* Don't believe everything it suggests to you. Our goal is to take over that voice through inner discipline so that you can speak to yourself like a cheerleader or most devoted fan!

Sadly, we've been conditioned to constantly downgrade ourselves, starting with our mind and words. Before we even give ourselves a chance to express what we desire or receive our good thoughts, we are surrounded with *"Who am I to be…"*, *"I'm not perfect yet"*, *"that's too much for me"* and so on and on. Nothing is <<too much>> for your purpose AND for your GOD.

The most attractive feature of the woman in her feminine essence is the radiance of her heart. Her willingness to surrender, give and receive love. That's divinely sexy. What makes her so, is awakened consciousness. In this chapter, my intention is to awake you take all your power back and make that first step into your Queen's mindset.

It takes an inner shift in the way you think about yourself and how you show up in the world to reveal your feminine presence. The transformation will be reflected in the way you speak, talk and live your life. The excellence of your spirit will become clearly visible to the outside world.

You're defined when things go wrong. And still, you rise.
You're defined when you're afraid. And you still go for it.
You're defined when you don't know how. And still, you find a way.

THE DEFINITION OF A QUEEN

A Queen represents the perfect example of class in a woman. She's the ultimate feminine role model in her category. Her energy represents and connects you with the highest expression of your soul. With your inner truth.
In the words of the author, Osmara Vindel, *archetypes are the embodiment of collective personality traits and personas we all share*. They're like the timeless characters we've seen on stage or tv throughout our lives.

A woman embodying her Queen archetype displays dignified, magnificent energy, which makes her a powerful and magnetic force to be reckoned with.

The queen is wise because she has learned from her mistakes and faced her inner demons. She has looked deep within herself and, as a result, she has become stronger.

She has a strong sense of duty and responsibility for the power bestowed upon her. Humble, yet, majestic. Possessing deep confidence and wisdom, not because of her external value, but because of who she is within. A strategic thinker and doer. Somewhat isolated – as she cannot be accessible to all those who desire to be in her presence all of the time.

Q Quality woman
U Ultimate presence
E Exceptional character
E Empowered internally
N No drama attitude

A Queen is a woman of quality and substance. Such quality starts with our thoughts, then the expression of them through speech and behaviour. When a Queen opens her mouth, everyone wishes to listen to her. Her words are pearls of wisdom.

A Queen won't show up below a certain standard, won't entertain low-quality conversations or behave in a way that isn't worthy of a Queen. Things that will get her attention are only those that deserve her attention. The reason why this is important is that without quality and substance deep within you, at your core, your authentic power won't have the impact or be compassionate enough for the task of serving your community.

An example of such quality is the American billionaire and TV, presenter Oprah Winfrey with her "SuperSoul Sunday" sessions as a way of bringing a soulful and elevating communication of quality and substance to mainstream media. Oprah thrives on using her gifts of power and generosity to open doors and possibilities for a new life for others. From her come these words of affirmation and inspiration: *"Think like a queen. A queen is not afraid to fail. Failure is another stepping-stone to greatness."*

Queens possess the ultimate presence. It emanates from the understanding of who you are and why you exist. From the confidence that knowing brings. A Queen's presence is the reflection of her excellent spirit. That noticeable quality of presence is the result of what she had the courage to say yes to in her life, and of the beliefs she stands for.

In this context, presence stands not so much about being physically present in the space, but rather the power to fill that space with your magnificent aura. Queens visibly stand out from the crowd just by being themselves, without the need to be over or underdressed. A great example is one of my greatest icons, The QUEEN OF HEARTS — PRINCESS DIANA.

As a woman, she had so many different roles: one of a loving mother, an independent woman, a fashion icon or an example and inspiration for millions of people. She didn't use the gift of her presence and status for personal benefit. She used it to make a change for a better world. Her presence brought hope to the hopeless on practically every given occasion.

This beautiful Princess told us *"I think the biggest disease the world suffers from in this day and age is the disease of people feeling unloved. I know that I can give love for a minute, for half an hour, for a day, for a month, but I can give. I am very happy to do that, I want to do that."* And she did, for far too short a time. Rest in Peace. You are forever beloved.

A Queen possesses excellent character. The Queen archetype is a masterful blend of both empowered feminine and masculine traits. That excellence is reflected in her daily choices, long-term decisions and the ability to see things through to completion. Traits like emotional maturity, kindness, ethics, loyalty, benevolence, patience, persistence and gentle strength definitely belong here. A Queen is always striving to improve her character and humble enough to rectify or make an apology. Her character is her single biggest asset which she builds her life upon and lays out her plans and visions. She banishes laziness, ignorance, dishonesty, and self-delusion. The importance of your character is a game-changer. Without its development, you won't be able to express the real you — and will instead give up on your desires when things get more challenging.

The correct character will make you carry on when others give up, help you keep your cool when others despair and allow you to keep believing in yourself when others have doubted.

Great examples of such are Madonna and Beyonce. It impacts every aspect of their lives and results, stronger than any adversity they have had to endure through their own journeys of self-mastery to the very top.

Empowered internally

The power of the Queen lies in her heart of courage. When facing a relationship disappointment, being challenged financially or dealing with adversity, Queens don't shrink and remove themselves from the game due to fear or self-doubt. They empower themselves from within to push through any resistance or setback.

What does it mean to be empowered from within?

"Between stimulus and response, there is a space. In that space is our power to choose our response. In our response lies our growth and our freedom."
—VIKTOR FRANKL, "MAN'S SEARCH FOR MEANING"

Most religions and philosophies depict the individual as rather dependant on external circumstances and the grace of luck. The power seems to be mostly placed outside the control of the individual. We seem to behave as if we were limited by the Higher Will. At least, the general public seems to have such an opinion.

The universe and the spiritual force (God, Spirit, The Quantum Field) is limitless. It has no limits. It can become anything and permeates everything. Here comes the greatest "aha" moment — even if you divide an infinite energy source into separate parts, each part still keeps that infinite power within.

Being empowered means accepting yourself as having ALL the power within you.

That means to firstly seek answers within your soul and check in with your intuition or God without blaming others. A Queen may well have a wise circle of advisors and experts, yet she remembers to think for herself. It means to not give away your power nor the responsibility for the creator of your outcomes, to your coach, mentor or your mother. A Queen is able to quickly elevate herself from a low emotional state or bad performance thanks to her agile self-awareness and mental discipline without being *too needy or desperate for others*. Also, one helpful quality that contributes to self-awareness is having a sense of humour about oneself and being balanced enough to turn a stressful situation into a comic one.

Through this understanding, we can draw these conclusions:

- Nothing is going to happen without you choosing it and claiming it: first mentally, then emotionally and physically. You must develop moment to moment emotional awareness — becoming aware of what kind of emotions are flowing through your body and keep asking yourself: "How do I choose to feel right now?"

- You have created and attracted everything that has happened so far in your life through your thoughts and emotional patterns, as well as your past choices. In most cases, you simply reacted to events according to your childhood programming, trying to keep yourself protected and avoid anything that you subconsciously associated with pain: a surplus of money, being in a relationship, being sensual or being seen and recognised publicly.

- You are the only one who can define the meaning of any experience: either empowering or a disempowering one.

- There are no victims nor culprits — just people who refuse to take full responsibility for their external outcomes by changing their internal perceptions. They are unconscious of their default emotional reactions. Every time you declare yourself as a powerless victim when facing a challenging situation, you deny your divine power to create your reality. You still create the experience but don't take responsibility for it by apportioning it to the actions of someone else.

- Your energy is projected and emitted through your beliefs and emotions: both representing the creative forces of either fear or love. So if you're afraid something may happen, its most probably to experiencing a previous similar experience -- as both fear and love are focused energy that brings about the people, situations, and events that match their vibration.

I'm being blunt with you here. Things we don't face become our limits. The worst kind of blindness is when we refuse to see.

So let's consider what you can do to empower yourself from within.

A Queen only asks questions that empower her, such as:

"What's the solution here?
How CAN I? How CAN I make this happen?
What is the truth about this situation? What's the lesson here? How can I overcome this challenge?
How can I take responsibility here?

— they're able to quickly course-correct, draw conclusions and move on fast.

Queens are victims of nothing and no one. They proclaim self-responsibility while at the same time being open to support, provision and protection.

Let's move on now to the last component of a Queen's mentality: No drama attitude. A Queen controls her mind and her emotions. This allows her to avoid self-induced problems like overthinking and overreacting. Queens don't freak out, panic or start shouting in public. She's able to take a moment to stop, take a moment to compose herself and respond appropriately, like the wise woman she is.

An example of that would be the attitude of the UK Primer Minister, Margaret Thatcher, A Queen Leader and famously known as the Iron Lady.

What we can learn from Lady Thatcher is to manage our emotional state in order to gain authority and trust. If you overcome fear and keep going in the face of criticism, you can achieve things that others have decided are impossible. The reason why 'no drama attitude' is so key to you being the Queen is that emotionally unstable women can't be trusted with power and responsibility. Only those that demonstrate the emotional maturity to confront challenges and situations will be promoted to a higher status.

Great! Now that you know the definition of the Queen, found out what it means to be empowered from within and the key features of a Queen mindset, I'd like to also help you by presenting a sharp contrast — Your Non-Queen.

WHAT A QUEEN IS NOT - MEET YOUR NON-QUEEN

The Non- Queen within you is that identity or part of your self that keeps you out of the game, tolerates less than you deserve, and operates way below your potential. You get the idea.

The reason why we must shed some light on your non-Queen-ly way of being because she's sneaky and smart. She talks you out of your dreams. She persuades you to give up before you even start and can sneak in at the least expected moment to ruin the whole party. I don't want you to be under the influence and sweet lies of your non-Queen.

I also want you to become aware at this stage that the journey from the 'wounded feminine' to an empowered feminine Queen — is about healing your relationship with the Masculine and how graciously you're able to receive. It's about being available to the greatness that men and masculine structures have to offer. It's also about how confident and worthy we feel to receive love, support, and abundance in your life.

If you want to know more, I speak about it in much greater depth in my first book **The Rich Soul**[1] , which I recommend to you if you haven't read it yet, to help overcome that money repelling torture, establish a supportive relationship with money and be spiritually and financially abundant in your life.

Below I will outline details of a few non Queen examples - The Little Girl, The Cinderella, and The Princess, so you have a more in-depth idea, identify which pattern shows up in your personal case and ultimately, transform your Non-Queenly traits.

Just so you know, it's quite common to have more than one non-Queenly way of being in different areas of your life. For example, you can be a Little Girl in your relationship and the Princess when it comes to your professional life. The purpose of getting to know your Non-Queen is to recognise her when she's stepped in unwanted, and let the real Queen take over.

WHEN YOU KNOW BETTER, YOU DO BETTER

THE LITTLE GIRL

---

1   The Rich Soul" — you can get it on Amazon from this link: or directly from my website at justinacarmo.com/richsoul

The first non Queenly archetype I observed through my experience with my private clients and while working with groups of women is **The Little Girl.**

Women would often complain about her in this way: *"I'd like to but… I sometimes feel like a helpless Little Girl, that just doesn't seem to be capable of doing anything about it"*.

A woman at this stage lives mainly unconscious to her thoughts, emotions, and desires. She usually overreacts to the stress triggers and feels helpless when confronted with adversities. She's unaware of the default programming dictating her behaviour. Despite being an adult, the wounded parts of herself make her behave both like a naive little girl, throwing emotional tantrums and a financial one, avoiding responsibility at all costs. She allows others to dictate her life experiences and postpones the necessary, yet often painful, transformation.

Internally, she feels abandoned, threatened or even emotionally orphaned by her mother and is inhibited by her demands.

The second non-Queenly type is the one that we know well from our childhood bedtime stories, **Cinderella.**

A woman in her **Cinderella** stage will do anything for approval and has no defined standards. She will give freely yet is unable to receive freely. She used her sexuality as a way to manipulate men or prove her worth, without valuing it as sacred.

She lives in self-denial, still limited by the wounds of the past she has yet to heal from. Her focus is to survive as she lives in a constant 'never enough pattern and craves to find a place where she could feel safe and finally belong. She doesn't consider herself worthy of deep love as she feels inferior and inadequate in some way.

Many modern women are frequently affected by the third non-Queen type, namely, **Princess**. Dependent and needy. The princess behaves sweet and innocent. May come across as 'spoiled' because of her attitude of entitlement. Often lacks gratitude and appreciation. Wants to be admired but is not ready yet to be of service herself and instead waits for her Prince Charming to save her. Her potential is dormant until awakened by a life crisis or tough, challenging time. Only then does she have the opportunity to transform into the Queen, if brave enough to take it.

PRINCESS	QUEEN
Confused	Focused
Quits	Perseveres
Indecisive	Decisive
Excuses	Zero Excuses
Fearful	Bold
Small Thinking	Big Thinking
Looks for approval	Self-assured

So, how to start thinking as a Queen?

Accepting and understanding why you adopted the traits of a particular type or types can help you heal what is screaming to be healed, so that you may become the highest, most potent version of yourself.

Stepping into your Queen consciousness means leaving behind the victim mentality: withholding, needy, dramatic, downgrading yourself, co-dependent, over-sensitive and over-emotional.

You start thinking as a Queen the moment you become awake to the fact that you are one. You admit Her presence deep within you and allow her expression on the outside. You begin to acknowledge her after all those years or even decades of repressing her. You take a deep breath and drop your shoulders. Even though your bank account might be far from royal or your life circumstances less tan majestic, the change has begun.

You're becoming a Queen and I'm so excited for you! So let's continue with your royal training…

CROWN ADJUSTING EXERCISES

EXERCISE #1: **Meeting your NON-Queen:**

After reading about non-Queenly types, you're now familiar with the charácter of your disempowered feminine side. The purpose of this exercise is to prevent your non-Queen from taking you out of the game and missing your biggest destiny:

Take the next page in this book and draw your non- Queen. Imagine that version of you that keeps you disempowered, feeling powerless and keeps you away from your desires.

Think deeply and clearly:

1. What's the message/visual of your non-Queen
2. Make contact with her and visualise her profile, draw that entity that's robbing you of your truth, your power, your destiny, everything you're capable of, the one running your life.
3. Become clear on who she is, visualise her, get the message of who this demon is, what does it look like, what is it saying to you. Draw out what you're hearing and seeing. Journal on your 'aha' moments and any recurring patterns that showed up in this exercise.

EXERCISE #2: **Reveal your QUEEN Within:**

Now, let's explore your current patterns and paradigm.
What stops you from empowering yourself to be the Queen?

List 10 specific ways in which you are not living like a Queen:

1.
2.
3.
4.
5.
6.
7.
8.
9.
10

List 10 Ways you're scared to live like a Queen:
(Below are some examples to give you an idea)
   a) Scared to be judged vain or that I'm wasting money
   b) Scared to just go for it, leap and commit 100%
   c) Not being bold, in it to win it, scared of really being seen
      as your true self
   d) Breaking my paradigm for once and for all

1.
2.
3.
4.
5.
6.
7.
8.
9.
10

BEST PRACTICES TO IMPLEMENT RIGHT AWAY:

A.**Empower yourself through WORDS.** Allow your words to honour you and your efforts. Let your words be kind, gentle and respectful, firstly towards yourself. Avoid the harsh statements that undermine you or downgrade you.

B. **Empower yourself through CHOICES.** When making a decision, begin to truly consider yourself, your own happiness and your soul — where previously you may just have been passive, ask yourself: "What do I really, really, really WANT here?"

C. **Empower yourself through FOCUS.** What deserves your attention, gets it. What doesn't deserve your attention gets ignored. Respect yourself enough to not entertain vain gossip, avoid negative social media input and direct your thoughts towards your most desirable outcomes and things that truly bring you pleasure.

Chapter Two

QUEENS LOVE PROGRESS

"A master does not shrink away from challenges but welcomes them. She looks the challenge in the eye and says "my soul's bigger than this". You came to teach me lessons in mastery. You came to show me I'm capable of so much more. You came to bless me — for I must rise up and confront you. And I will. And I will even surprise myself by what I am capable of overcoming and in what innovative and amazing ways I can transcend old patterns".
— UNKNOWN

In chess, the Queen figure is the most powerful piece. She can move in any straight direction — forward, backward, sideways, or even diagonally - as far as possible. Likewise, in life, a woman awakened to a Queen consciousness is all about growth and strategic course-correcting in order to move forward. Such a woman craves progress in all areas of her life.

A QUEEN KNOWS ONLY ONE DIRECTION: FORWARD.

Often times, the situation she's in can challenge her emotionally or even try to tempt her to just conform with the status quo of others around her — yet she is unapologetic about expanding her contribution, status, and realm she's creating.

Advancing despite fear and adversities requires a lot of spiritual courage. Courage is a conscious act of refusing to remain in fear. The challenge here consists in overcoming your old patterns of withdrawing emotionally when triggered, hiding when exposed, staying scared around your finances or keep shutting down your heart in an act of self-protection.

With the Queen's courage, she's more than willing to do what it takes to break through to a new level and achieve progress in her life. To meet her fears head on — and smash through them. To confront the truth about her financial decisions, get over herself and make up for it. To challenge an old part of her personality that resists the very thing she desires. To speak her truth lovingly and commit to taking actions in line with her goals, and see them through until completion.

The opposite of growth and progress is inertia and stagnation. In this state you passively conform to the outer reality, reacting to it instead of consciously co-creating with the universe. You create inertia when day after day, month after month you keep reacting with the same emotions (often unconscious) of discontent and frustration – it becomes habit-forming...the norm.

On the other hand, you co-create by drawing into the present moment the emotions and mental state of the future you that you are seeking to become. Eg peace, clarity and a sense of being provided for around your money.

In order to change your reality, you have to ignore your reality for some time.

I don't mean here that you should become completely out of touch with it! At any given moment we can either scare ourselves due to learned behaviour, or detach from them and soothe ourselves with peaceful thoughts. You have a choice. If we follow the first, our body will produce a stress reaction and feelings of fear and anxiety will appear. Such emotional states simply feel more familiar to us as we've been conditioned to living in fear in many areas of our lives. More than that, our bodies crave the emotional chemistry of such states. We have to unplug ourselves from these old emotions and install new ones.

"You can't go into your future with the biology of your past"
—DR. JOE DISPENZA

So rather, you simply stop reacting to situations and issues with old complaining thoughts and instead, begin to embody the new feelings of peace, joy and gratitude and thoughts of safety, love, and connection with God.

You can't generate wealth, carrying over thoughts of lack and feelings of panic.

You can't generate love, carrying over thoughts of resentment or blame and feelings of sadness and abandonment.

You can't generate a beautiful body, carrying over thoughts of harsh self-punishment and criticism and feelings of disgust, inadequacy, and insecurity.

We block our progress as wise and smart women by telling ourselves disempowering stories of how we're simply not good enough (yet) and thinking we deserve no better than this. By believing that we're unable to rise beyond the problem that has been holding us back we give away our power to even try. As a result, we end up feeling inadequate for the purpose God has designed us for. We fall into extremes thinking we're either "too little" or wanting "too much".

Have you ever been labelled as "too much"? Wanting too much, speaking too much or being too much? I'm sure you must have. I need to remind you:

NOTHING IS TOO MUCH FOR YOU AND YOUR GOD.

The universe has been preparing you for this elevation in your consciousness. For stepping up and into your fullest soul expression.

Nothing about you is random. In the past, you might have been seeking blame everywhere for your messed up childhood, problematic experience with your parents, you're less than perfect looks or wobbly financial issues. I get it.

It's time we uncover the truth about your destiny: you've been created 100% bespoke for the unique mission by God that you and ONLY you can fulfill, totally on purpose. God doesn't make mistakes.

Starting from your looks, your origins, your family, cultural background and ending on your life struggles and obstacles — all of that represents your inner resources and was meant to train your spiritual resilience. At times it must have been so hard and so inhumanly tough for you to overcome life punches, but hey…what if all that you've been through, has been preparing you for the very things you asked for?

You've been fully equipped since you were born to fulfill your purpose. You're fully loaded in order to succeed. You were made perfect for your unique purpose. However, when you deny yourself, diminish your mission in the world, (or abandon it completely through fear) — you're also denying GOD.

If you're denying yourself, your growth and your talents — you're denying your Creator.

You actually block all the blessings the generous universe has lined up for you. All the possibilities, supportive people and miracles. In a desperate craving for approval, we may even sacrifice our unique way of being in the world in order to please others.

YOU DON'T HAVE TO PLEASE OTHERS.
PLEASE GOD.

So let's set an intention to make peace with your tumultuous past then, shall we?

We find ourselves unable to choose a clear action plan and go for it. Instead, we tolerate what we think we deserve. From my observations, way too many women nowadays have a too high tolerance for pain, exhaustion and unnecessary discomfort in their lives.

Have you ever resisted your own progress because of the fear of the unknown and hesitancy of moving forward? Have you spent your time keeping all your joys and desires on hold? Waiting and waiting for things to change on their own in order to live your best life *one day when…*? And lastly, have you ever felt fed up with holding yourself back from the very thing you knew you should do?

We've all been there.

We've listened to the voices of our inner coward instead of our Queen. Instead of waking up from the lethargy and actually doing something radical to transform our bank account situation, business mistakes or our body — we've put up with stagnation for way too long, simply getting used to its deteriorating condition. It cost us money, years of our youth and our emotional health.

And then one day you decide to draw a line, that enough is enough and you make a clear cut decision — it's done. It's **over!**

My intention for our time together in this chapter is that having now made that decisión, you'll begin to get yourself out of any delusion or lethargy you might be currently going through in your life or that used to keep you stuck.

I will teach you what it means to **"Be a Queen about it"** and how to empower yourself to take actions that raise both your standards and your results.

Ready to bust through some of the old blocks that used to keep you in the same place for years? Let's get down to our transformative work together!

STRONGER THAN EXCUSES, BIGGER THAN THE FEAR

First, I'd like you to pay attention to how your inner talk creates your outer world.

Most of the time, what keeps you stuck is your inner critic, demanding perfection. My solution? Adopt a "do it anyway" policy. Teach yourself the habit of taking actions for the right reasons, even though they may be imperfect, one by one. Build momentum on your imperfections and keep practicing them as you move forward. Scared? Good. Do it anyway. Bad hair day? Good. Do it anyway. Don't feel like it? Good. Do it anyway.

DON'T FEAR NOT BEING PERFECT. FEAR NOT BEING ON PURPOSE

I'd rather have you take 10 steps wrong than overanalysing taking one step right, while somebody is waiting to be served and inspired by you. While somebody is yearning for your presence. While somebody is praying for someone like you to show up in their life.

FEARS YOU DON'T FACE BECOME YOUR LIMITS

Let's demystify now some versions of our inner voices: **The Coward and the Saboteur.**

THE COWARD

The coward is the passive polar opposite of your true heroine self. A woman under the control of the coward lacks courage and holds back her initiative. She avoids confrontation and has no strength to stand up for herself.

I admit it. I've been a coward plenty of times in my own life. I used to withdraw emotionally. I denied myself my own voice in the world and was scared to the bone of revealing my books to the world.

The coward protects the fearful and frightened parts of our personality. It keeps us in a place where we remain less than we're meant to be and blocks the intimacy we're meant to experience.

The internationally renowned author, Gary Zukav teaches that the frightened parts of our personality cause our pain of powerlessness, isolation, and separation. The potential within us that cannot break through the layers and layers of fear over time becomes a frustration, resentment, hopelessness, and anger.

Therefore, never allow the coward to dissuade you or discourage you as it's purpose is to delay and disempower you with its soft and dissuasive lies:

"I'm not ready yet"
"I'm not prepared enough"
"I haven't got time"
"I just don't know how"
"I will do it later"

THE SABOTEUR

The Saboteur within us the most fearful of change, especially if that change is going to potentially change your entire life. It loves withdrawing from commitments at the last minute or giving up on something even when tonnes of work and preparation has already been invested.

It's triggered by our inner fears of surviving in the hear and now and getting ahead. It resists the breakthrough to a new level because it feels much more comfortable with the same old story of struggling but belonging.

When your inner Saboteur overpowers you it can cause you to lose opportunities, waste money or close your heart. It manipulates you with doubts about not being able to pay your bills, losing your stable job. It tells you that you're not good enough for your dream relationship.

It is a master at making up dramatic stories that have little to do with reality but cause you to doubt your instincts. Over time, the Saboteur will try to push you away from any people, places that situations that could make you joyful with the inner dialogue like this:

"What if it doesn't work?"
"What's the point?"
"What if I fail?"
"What if it's not worth my time/ effort/ money?"
"What if I'm making a mistake?"

THE WARRIORESS

Do you need to call on your inner warrioress in order to move forward?

As a little girl, I was fascinated by the figure of Xena, the Warrior Princess. I admired her fearlessness, feminine courage and her ability to express and concentrate her anger to fight for a just cause.

The lesson that warrioresses hold for us is that delving into our femininity doesn't mean becoming defenceless or repressing our strength. Just the opposite. B by being prudent, alert and aware of any potential danger I show we become stronger. The warrioress doesn't give up in through panic or being overwhelmed. She fights back. Kicks ass!
The energy of our inner warrior allows us to reconnect with our healthy instincts: not putting up with mistreatment, chronic self-sacrifice or being humiliated. She protects our boundaries and gives us the courage to finally fight for the right solutions to our problems.

When we activate and take on the energy of this spirit within ourselves, we're able to reclaim our power to combat adversity, feel grounded and courageous. She allows us to gain strength and rise up after the biggest failures. She keeps going despite the wounds and takes a giant, trusting and courageous leap forward, towards what's meant for us.

There is a warrioress within all of us. Use her to create positive lifestyle habits that protect your energy levels and create emotional harmony. To enjoy the good times and work through the more challenging ones. If your project collapses, begin work on another. If a relationship fails, grow from it and develop another one. Outline your work. Plan. Move steadily towards the goal. Persuade ALL parts of your mind and soul to pursue your dream.

Allow your inner warrioress to speak her voice:

"This is what we are doing. You are going to help me. There's to be no argument and no discussion. You have made a decision and that's the end of the matter."

CROWN ADJUSTING EXERCISES:

1. Identify which non-Queen type (the Coward or the Saboteur) makes you lose your power? In what specific way? How does it make you act in your life? Write below.

2. What's the boldest action that I can take to make my desire real?

3. What am I afraid to do but know that I should?

Chapter Three

QUEENS DO THE WORK

"You're being presented with a CHOICE: evolve or keep suffering.
If you choose to remain unchanged, you will experience the same
challenges, the same routine, the same storms, the same situations
and the same pain, until you learn from them.

Until you love yourself enough to say "no more".
Until you choose change. You'll be given everything you need
Choose to evolve."

— CREIG CRIPPEN

It's shocking how much pain we can put up with for the sake of staying in our comfort zone. Yet the valley you fear to enter, holds the treasure you seek.

I see many entrepreneurs being willing to accept to months of zero income in their business. Smart women overstaying for years in failed relationships. Others who just helplessly surrendered to being in debt instead of fiercely increasing their income, or the most talented people I know, hiding their superpowers just because they were taught to stay in the middle.

A QUEEN INSISTS ON HER BREAKTHROUGH

Luckily, every pain has a tipping point, the moment when it becomes unbearable. The moment when you're just DONE with being hurt and realise that this pain makes no more sense. Later, you'll know you'd rather grow through joy and love from now on instead of pain and fear - how much easier it would have been to release that pain if you'd paid attention to it from the beginning.

One thing is clear. Self-torture and masochism belong to the Middle Ages. Not to our 21st century. Struggle and suffering are optional. There is no need to dignify it anymore. No prizes are given for the *"Best Martyr of the Year"*.

Life's meant to be purposeful, fun and joyful. Seek pleasure in moving forward. Allow yourself to enjoy the journey of becoming. Make it worth your smile and a completely open heart.

You're always just ONE decision away from a totally different life, but that decision involves commitment. Stop resisting it.

You wait, afraid to commit, thinking that this may hurt you. No! It's the very thing that builds you up. ONE decision away from a totally different life. Keep asking yourself *"How committed am I to this dream? How committed am I?* Let the answer heal you. Examine your fears and embrace your courage.

What fears are standing in your way? Where did you get these fears from? From family or friends? Give your fear a colour. Then give your courage a colour. Which is the brightest?

List three things you can do to overcome the blocks that the coward holds over you.

1. ____
2. ____
3. ____

Break them down into small steps to begin changing your relationship from one of fear to one of faith.

A PROGRESSIVE MIND KEEPS ASKING "HOW CAN I?"

Your mind is such an incredible asset in life. Your most precious real estate. You have to start owning its space — because no thought lives in your mind rent-free. Each thought has a consequence. That means you have to train yourself to become more and more aware to what kind of thoughts you're allowing to pass through your mind.

There's no place for mental laziness in a Queen's mind.

She is fierce and unapologetic about only entertaining thoughts that empower her self-worth, self-belief, and capacity to succeed on her own terms. She catches them in an instant and replaces them with thoughts that add to her strength and reflect God's truth about her. She has trained herself to move away from the unconscious fearful reactions that used to scare her. Instead, she practices feeling the way she truly wants to feel, whatever the circumstances. She calls in feelings of peace, love and being supported and provided for.

A woman finds herself being stuck and held in her life when she becomes mentally lazy, allowing external circumstances or others to control her emotional reactions. To push her buttons.

A BREAKTHROUGH REQUIRES A TRUE DECISION FOLLOWED BY ACTION

What does it mean to decide truly? It means to cut <u>ANY</u> other option. To become unavailable to any other alternative from the one you choose. To make a true decision is to follow it with ACTION, FOCUS, and DEDICATION.

When I used to hear my mentors tell me *"You haven't decided yet"* or *"It's because you haven't made a real decision yet"*, my rebel soul used to get so irritated. *"Why haven't I?"* — I used to think.

The key here is you DECIDING from the bottom of your GUT. You making the BOLD statement within your SOUL that this-is-IT. You're completely unavailable for being overdrawn on your account, zero income months in your business or just not fitting your favourite dress. Not a second longer will you perpetuate this state of being. That a NEW ERA begins HERE and NOW.

Be strong enough to decide! You've been avoiding that decision for years now. Nothing gets better just by waiting. Everything gets better by truly COMMITTING to making it so.

YOUR HAPPINESS DEPENDS 100% ON YOUR MENTAL DISCIPLINE + EMOTIONAL STATE

A mediocre mind will always have excuses to avoid action. It's addicted to its well-known and comfortable inertia — be it depleted finances, a ruined sentimental life or life-long overweight and physical neglect. And that's so not you. Such a mind is invested in keeping things as they are, despite the long-term devastation it causes and resisting what it could become and create.

When we're afraid to move forward, we deny our true calling — our soul's Truth. To compensate, we mask that fear with distractions such as our phones, YouTube, or Facebook, because behind compulsive distractions lies fear. The ultimate fear to be who we're meant to be — the Queens of our divine life.

A Queen refuses to accept mediocrity in her own thinking, demeanour, and behaviour. She's above and beyond her own limiting stories but instead, committed to maximising her own potential.

That's why a much more Queenly approach here consists of being carefully selective with the way you think about yourself and practicing emotional awareness moment to moment.

This means being aware of the emotional states you experience and flow through your body (sadness, fear, anger, etc), and then making a conscious choice of how you actually want to feel.

You have to learn to banish from your mind the severe, attacking and criticising thoughts about yourself. And this takes inner work to control your mental focus.

SAME THOUGHTS + SAME EMOTIONS = SAME RESULTS
NEW THOUGHTS + NEW EMOTIONS = NEW RESULTS

Let me give you an example of how this would look like in practical terms:

Let's say you found yourself in a difficult financial situation and short of money for way too longer than you can afford to be (hello, who hasn't been there?!).

As you see less and less money in your bank account as a result of past choices and thoughts, you begin to feel insecure, anxious or fearful (old emotions you've been conditioned to feel around money). As a result, you continue to scare yourself with a vision of a future that only makes you feel worse.

What would a Queen do instead?

#Queen's #1 Rule
A Queen knows only one direction — FORWARD

She's alert. She's in touch with her instincts. She is always ready to course correct. Her progress is non-negotiable. Therefore, even in such challenging circumstances, she elevates her consciousness above her problems. She has learned to control her feelings and practice the emotional state she wants to experience. She made herself only available to feel peaceful and provided for around her finances. She doesn't freak out or panic.

By the power of intention, she calls back her power. She's eager to find solutions for herself without collapsing into unnecessary dramas. A Queen knows old thoughts will only bring about more of the same. So she beings to plant in her mind prosperous and empowering thoughts and through that, bring about a different emotion — the one of peace and safety. As a result of her state of being (the combination of her thoughts + emotions), she is in a position to calmly consider practical options and implement them quickly: *what savings can I make on my monthly expenditure? I will seek financial advice to help solve this. Do I have anything of value that I no longer need or want?*

BEING A QUEEN ABOUT IT

She's a Queen about it. That means she's 100% responsible and she's the one creating her outcomes, for good or bad. It also means to confront the facts with dignity head-on, instead of hiding or avoiding. By the power of intention, she chooses to shift her perception from the one of fear to love. To no longer be scared but peaceful instead. And because of that, she chooses to show up and to be bigger than her circumstances, not fall prey to them.

A woman with a Queen's consciousness keeps asking herself questions that expand her creativity and build her inner resilience. Her inner self-talk is healthy and reinforcing. In contrast, a woman with a broken consciousness will torture herself deep inside with constant blaming, punishing thoughts and scaring herself with images of future failures. We all can do much better than this. Let's be Queens about it.

CROWN ADJUSTING EXERCISES:

Consider these two empowering questions:

1. *What do I really, really, desire now in this situation?*
2. *God/ Soul/ Universe what would you have me do now?*

Take your diary and a pen. Then a deep breath. Place your hand on your heart. Connect with it. Allow the answers to come to you one by one.

The first question focuses on your desired outcome instead of dwelling upon the problem that keeps you paralysed. The second question releases you from the pity-party and empowers you to receive divine guidance.

Whenever you find yourself doubting how far you can go, just remember how far you have come

3. Queenly identity — Think about your goal and obstacle you want to overcome. Can you think of a woman who has successfully achieved something similar as an example? Then ask yourself: Who is the woman I choose to embody today?

Examples:

— The woman who can make tough, challenging decisions
— The woman who keeps the promises she made to herself in the morning
— The woman who takes care of herself emotionally and physically
— The woman who uses her time effectively

Raise up your standards — raise your results.

4. i) Asking your Queen Within:

My Queen Within, please speak up. What do you want to tell me?

Example:

You are desirable. Value yourself to a royal standard. Make your decisions with dignity. Serve your best. Serve your greatest. Speak words of love, compassion and encouragement.

ii) Meditation with your Queen Within:

I'm so ready now to move forward. I am so ready NOW. As a Queen, I am proud of my progress and how far I've come.
I grace people with my beauty and my value.

DON'T QUIT

When things go wrong, as they sometimes will,
When the road you're trudging seems all uphill,
When the funds are low and the debts are high,
And you want to smile, but you have to sigh,
When care is pressing you down a bit,
Rest, if you must, but don't you quit.

Life is queer with its twist and turns,
As every one of us sometimes learns,
And many a failure turns about,
When he might have won had he stuck to it out;
Don't give up though the pace seems slow,
You may succeed with another blow.

Success is failure turned inside out;
The silver tins of the clouds of doubt;
And you can never tell how close you are,
It may be near when it seems far;
So stick to the fight when you're hardest hit,
It's then things seem worst that you must not quit.

— RUDYARD KIPLING

Chapter Four

QUEENS POSITION THEMSELVES FOR GREATNESS

"At every moment, a woman makes a choice:
between the state of the queen and the state of the slave girl.
In our natural state, we are glorious beings. In the world of illu-
sion, we are lost and imprisoned, slaves to our appetites and our
will to false power. Our jailer is a three-headed monster--one head
our past, one our insecurity, and one our popular culture."
— MARIANNE WILLIAMSON

You ARE called to greatness. You DO have a magnificent destiny in your life. You CAN overcome your biggest challenges. "Good enough" is not your destiny. Greatness is.

You were created to live a life of joy and happiness. A life that your soul can be proud of. You were created to break the generational curses. And set yourself and your people free.

The reason you find it hard to believe you're capable of great things is that society has taken great care to ensure you've had enough attacks, setbacks, pain, and rejections that you question yourself.

It's time to let go of the burden of everything that didn't turn out as you had hoped. Accept the reality that these things happened, but don't let them poison your energy anymore.

It's high time to forgive any of your disappointments and focus on reaching forward — towards the innate greatness that God has destined you for.

Maybe too many setbacks on your way have weakened your drive. Maybe you've just lost confidence to make things happen. It doesn't matter…

Now, you might be at the stage in life where after all those setbacks you've just begun to play it safe and been putting up with a mediocre vision for your life. So have a think, what's the dream that you worked on for so long and gave up on?

____

____

Time to stir up that dream within you again! Admit, don't you still desire it? The truth is, deep inside your heart is still yearning for more love, more excitement, more adventure, and more contribution.

But Justina "I don't know how. I've tried so many times already and it didn't work out. I only got myself in trouble. I don't know what I'm doing wrong. I don't know how to even start again".
I hear you. Or to be more precise, I hear your ego playing a victim. Let me ask you, in such circumstances, are you using your imagination for good? Or are you creating for yourself a nightmare? It's important you become aware of what you're settling for.

When I myself used to moan like that, my wonderful Queen friend Alex used to wake me up to reality and say to me "Come on Justina, those who made it to the top DESERVED IT. They earned it. They grew stronger than their own mental and material limitations. They paid the price in full."

They were in it for the long haul. The greatest amongst us mastered the basics. Especially, the fact of maintaining unwavering faith in the face of adversities. So dig deep inside and say "I decide to rise. I've made up my mind. I'm not leaving it half-way or even 90% of the way. I will make it all the way through. I'm still in the game. I'm gonna do this until it's completed. I will see it through until its manifestation. I know God wouldn't forsake me and make me go through all of this in vain — the ultimate purpose is my victory".

Those words were like a cold shower to my ego, but they did empower my soul. As Queens, we must use our imagination to envision our aims, in order to become unstoppable in pursuit of greatness.

Moments like that are testing our faith and self-belief. As Joel Osteen preaches: "The good news is that just because you gave up on a dream, doesn't mean God gave up". God gave you beautiful desires, whispered promises to your spiritual listening, revealed a bigger and exciting vision for your life — it's our task to re-align with God again and rebuild our faith.

So my Queen, let's stop settling and begin to stretch.

What would you do if you were brave?

LEAVING FANTASY LAND

We've already discussed women playing small out of fear. They're afraid to really go for their dreams and stepping fully into their power, instead choosing to remain in the role of the Saboteur, The Little Girl or Cinderella

We go into fantasy land when we feel disempowered

The common pattern I observed both in my own life and in experiences with my clients is that when reality gets too overwhelming, we tend to escape into what I call "the fantasy land". The Neverland. The future utopia. What I mean by that is avoiding to face the current reality, grounding ourselves in practical solutions and taking a step by step approach towards problem-solving and our progress.

Instead, women keep spinning their wheels, set huge goals that too often are too big of a stretch both for their finances and their subconscious to believe it. Another version of the fantasy land is to keep waiting in paralysis by analysis that "one day…" things will simply get better by themselves. That's certainly where I wasn't "one day, Justina…" until I decided:
No more wishing. No more wanting. No more *one day*…

I was hoping that God, clients or friends would do for me what I wasn't doing for myself. That was to truly value my self-worth, to appreciate myself, and to provide for myself, not only financially but also spiritually and emotionally.

The price of living in fantasy land is initial naive enthusiasm that ends up with a bitter and painful disillusion. The huge disappointment of having invested all you had: your time, your savings and late nights and still coming up short in results. I saw that with women who hoped for a great relationship and were naive for way too long about the man they were dating. I saw that with women who crushed their businesses, hoping for a great revenue months after they over-invested in a mentor or a course, yet not subsequently taking personal responsibility for their financial situation.

What's the solution then? You are.

You are the rescuer.
You're gonna rescue yourself from your own version of mediocrity into your greatness.

Re-commit to your greatness.

CONSCIOUSLY ASK YOURSELF FOR MORE BRILLIANCE TO SURFACE

> 'The path to greatness begins with
> your willingness to take small steps.'
> — KATHY MCCLARY

That excellent vibration of a Queen is within you. You have access to it in every present moment, it's just been pushed to the far corners of your true self, remember her? The one who is resourceful and able to figure out the solution no matter what, as if your life depended on it.

Yes! We CAN be the Queen, we just have to rise above our insecurities. Easier said than done, sure. And you might be wondering how to connect with that innate greatness, in a way that doesn't won't make us bossy or overpowering. Truth is that each of us is work in progress as we claim our Queendom and it's not that you're the Queen and no one else is, we are all entitled to finding and claiming our own crown.

Look at you: You're educated, intelligent, pretty and friendly. You've been through so much. And you've overcome so many adversities. How come you don't realise how extremely capable and powerful you are? How come you don't realise that you do have the power to take the initiative and actually make that necessary breakthrough happen?

May this chapter be the key to your liberation.

WALK TALL, BABY!

We've been taught to think about ourselves as inferior and deficient in some way. This world is plagued by insecure women, focused on their perceived flaws. We've been conditioned to downgrade ourselves, our merits and skills.

You can quickly detect a woman's level of self-worth and self-respect just by listening to her words. How often do we hear women say "I'm so proud of myself", "I'm great at", "I appreciate myself" or "Well done me". Instead, we get "I'm struggling with", "I'm terrible at", "I'm so clumsy with". Have we forgotten that our self-talk becomes our reality? We must honour ourselves through our words and practice self-respect, gently noticing our progress instead of always being focused on our shortcomings.

We've also been taught to feel ashamed about our bodies and keep our self-esteem low. That's how whole industries manipulate women! Your task is to fall in love with the body that God gave you. Why? Because regardless of your size or looks, there is a wise and loving man who dreams precisely about what you represent, in mind and body, represent.

Negativity and insecurity never sit with brilliance, power, and prosperity.

My Dear Queen, decide you're not one of these insecure women any-more. You must refuse such a way of being in the world. If at any point in your life, you got scared, shy or insecure about yourself, know that such thoughts and states don't come from the Divine, from God. Actually, if it's not loving, it's not of God. It's not you. You've simply been conditioned to be insecure.

Insecurity is the mentality of behaving below our real potential and capacity. Such insecurity is a by-product of low-vibe and disempowering thoughts. Confront them. Question them one by one. Attack them. Your insecurities will never go away silently from your mind. You must banish them forcefully from your life. Refuse such programming, because they will only keep you in a prison of doubt and questioning yourself. And you're not anyone's victim. You're your own heroine.

God doesn't create junk. You're His Superstar. His A-Player.

Connect with that quiet, confident voice that says: "I CAN. I am able. I am a woman who can carry more power — in my life, around my money and in my contribution to the world" Humility, in turn, says: "I am also equal with everyone". It teaches that there's is nothing to be gained by feeling superior to others.

> The time for you to be an iconic woman is NOW.
> The time for you to be the Queen is NOW.

So here's how a Queen would avoid the trap of the "fantasy land":

It's simple. She becomes grounded about her body, her finances and commitments, instead of freestyle floating in the clouds. She embraces, as you must, whatever she's been resisting. Deals with what she's been avoiding. Tackles her fears. Re-commits.

You get out of the "fantasy land" by:

- Facing your money obligations head-on and with a resourceful "can-do attitude". What yo take action to deal with, gets done.

- Showing up and taking responsibility for your business consistently, if what you desire is to bring in more money

- Devote yourself to a committed relationship if what you desire is a loving partnership or a husband

- Commit to losing those extra kilos if what you desire is to feel great physically and taking pride in your appearance

- Finally, making that tough decision about what you desire with clarity and end the confusion

Someone once said to me:
"I don't know how you do it"

I told them
"I wasn't given a choice"

A Queen lives completely in her soul's truth, but, with her feet on the ground. Living in the "fantasy land" means only hoping, praying[2] and wishing.

She's in the now. It's foolish and naive to believe everything we're told by others. Discernment is key to choosing wisely and making key decisions in your life. As they say, a stitch in time saves nine.

Be clear and specific on what you desire and why. Unlike other women who make decisions frivolously based on their emotions, a Queen knows when to apply cold logic. She takes things one step at a time, calmly. A Queen knows that what expands or threatens her greatness is her moment to moment choices.

ON THE QUEST FOR SELF- ACTUALISATION

As you awake more and more to your Queenly consciousness, you will begin to feel the urge to manifest your full feminine potential. Ultimately, you're here on this planet to

---

2   I do believe in prayer, yet prayers without actions are just wishes.

express your genius and feminine gifts and care to the world in ways that make others thrive. By being a loving presence in the world. But in order to do that, you must let go of everything and everyone that holds you back from being and receiving your best from life.

That process is called self-actualisation. Queens live constantly upgrading their minds, way of being in the world and circle of influence. Women with the consciousness of a Queen are quick to course-correct in the present moment and rectify as soon as necessary. She's aware that if she maximises her life she'll positively impact the lives of other women around her too.

In turn, unconscious common women live trapped in the past. The consequences of not self-actualising is being trapped for decades in outdated and broken programming from our childhood, unhealed emotional trauma from past relationships, or spiritual immaturity.

SELF ACTUALISATION — the process of a woman upgrading her identity (beliefs about herself, her abilities and behaviour), into new elevated standards that reflect her current spiritual connection with God and willingness to be of greater, benevolent service to her family or community.

In order to self-actualise your consciousness as a woman, implement these 3 steps:

- Self-forgiveness (being able to release guilt and blame from your consciousness towards yourself)
- Self-assurance (being able to run on the energy created from the certainty of who you are, what you're capable of and what you're committed to)
- Re-connect with your vision (elevating your thinking, emotions, and actions above current circumstances in order to envision a new future that you will work relentlessly towards creating)

Let's take a look now at each step and how you can practically implement them into your life:

SELF- ASSURANCE

*"If I want something, I go get it.
Anything that I believe will stop me, I question."*
— BYRON KATIE

The former you would beg for some little attention or praise. We're addicted to being approved at all costs. We self-abandon our greatest dreams in order to please others and gain their approval. We wait to be given some permission and hear: "yes, now you can go for it", "yes, you're beautiful enough for me", "yes, you've got what it takes", as if we had to first delegate our creative power in order to decide what would make us happy, afraid to make a mistake.
You don't need someone else's permission to be yourself. A Queen is always self-assured. This means she checks in with her intuition. Her inner dialogue is self-empowering and doesn't depend on other people's opinions about her. She consults her God and her journal. She allows herself to follow the voice of her soul, even though sometimes it might be against the commonly accepted rules.

Don't get me wrong. I'm all about being respectful toward others and considering the wellbeing and preferences of those around me. It doesn't mean though that I'm waiting for permission to take action, or will play the martyr just because someone might not like me 'going for it'.

So let me ask you:

1. Think about a specific situation in your life where do you need to assure yourself about your power and abilities? What

do you expect other people to do for you in that situation? How can you do instead of what you expect from others?

FORGIVENESS

*"An open heart is a beginning of greatness.
It is an expression of humility. It is a foundation for the development of such virtues as prayer, faith, courage, contentment, happiness, love, and well-being."*
— JAMES E. FAUST

We hear a lot about the importance of forgiving those who have harmed us and it is essential in your journey that you do so. As is forgiving yourself.

The unwillingness to forgive makes a woman come across as bitter, frustrated and much less radiant and attractive than she really is. It's an expression of spiritual vanity and immaturity of her spirit. Our ego prefers to remain attached to the drama, self-punishment and recreates the inner conflict. Until we break this pattern of unconscious self-punishment and self-blaming this lack of forgiveness will block your income, intimacy and overall satisfaction in your life.

The true act of forgiveness comes from the depth of your soul.

So begin to awake to the fact that all peace begins with you. You're either a peace-maker or a conflict-maker. Which one are you being as in your heart of hearts? And which one would you rather be?

YOU DESERVE YOUR OWN FORGIVENESS.

I once heard Oprah Winfrey define forgiveness as never again using the past against someone. Likewise, self-forgiveness is about never again using your past mistakes against yourself.

It's about committing to doing your own hard work, confronting with brutal honesty the deeper forces at play which led you to make those mistakes in the first place. And then, to clean up your mess as best you can and recommitting yourself to do better next time. And when you mess up again (as you may do), to repeating this cycle.

If you've ever done something you regretted, then you're not alone. We all have. The reality is that everyone does stupid, selfish or apparently unforgivable things at times. I know I have. Like when I took too much of financial risk in my business and got myself in debt. Or when I didn't make it to my grandmother's funeral. Or when I hurt with my words the person I cared about the most. You get the idea.

Self-forgiveness is my monthly journalling practice where I take the time to free the mind of my past mistakes and frustrations. As these are the precise blocks of our 3rd chakra -- blocking our personal power and healthy self-esteem.

Below are some questions that will empower you. Take some to reflect on your (they will make for powerful healing!):

1. What do I keep blaming myself for? What event from my past still makes me feel guilty even though apparently it no longer should?
2. What do I need to forgive myself for?
3. Am I willing to accept my own responsibility for that event?
4. What's going to improve if I let go of that event and stop punishing myself because of it?

1. I release the guilt from my consciousness about ______
____
____ I
know now I'm innocent and I forgive myself my past decisions and that specific situation. I release that sensation of guilt and I completely forgive myself now. I am free.

2. I release the guilt from my consciousness about ______
____
____
I know now I'm innocent and I forgive myself my past decisions and that specific situation. I release that sensation of guilt and I completely forgive myself now. I am free.

3. I release the guilt from my consciousness about ______
____
____
I know now I'm innocent and I forgive myself my past decisions and that specific situation. I release that sensation of guilt and I completely forgive myself now. I am free.

4. I forgive myself for not making the improvements I swore I was devoted to, like ______________________________
____
____ I'm not
playing the martyr with myself over this issue anymore. I choose new intentions.

RE-CONNECT WITH YOUR VISION

*"It's all too easy to give up, to stop believing, to turn away from the
light. The evidence that the darkness will prevail is everywhere.
But I am not persuaded. Because my heart keeps opening, because
humans keep going, because the sun keeps rising. It may well be
that we make it through by the narrowest of margins, but we will.
"*

— JEFF BROWN

When you have lots of goals, inspired ideas, and competing
priorities, it's easy to get overwhelmed and frustrated. Thought's like "I'm a loser" or "I can't seem to get things done"
can try to invade your mind — your task is to not even entertain them in your head and immediately reverse them. As
Queens, we banish disempowering thoughts with no mercy.

In my experience, crazy passionate individuals are prone to
repeated cycles of inspiration and burnout. It starts with inspiration, which leads to excitement, and then to overwork
('cause you're so passionate about going after it), then
overwhelmed, frustration, fatigue, and eventually burn out.
That is until we find renewed inspiration and the cycle starts
over again!

Losing your drive or faith in your vision affects everyone differently. For some, it's feeling "worn down,", not wanting
to work, not enjoying or feeling that spark you once had for
your mission, etc. A common theme I often observed in my
clients is that they were missing that original excitement and
joy for what they were up to because of temporary setbacks.
They longed to turn the switch back on or find something
else that excited them even more. So, you can see why this
starts the cycle over again, and again, and again. Have you
experienced this?

Your vision falls apart because you stop trusting yourself. You need to cultivate a higher level of self-trust. If you don't, your lower-self will drag you down and destroy that vision you once had. So in moments of tests and trials, I reconnect with my vision and begin to repeat to myself words we all need to hear: "I trust myself. I trust the universe is working behind the scenes in my favor. I've got what it takes to accomplish this vision". I mean: "I'm gonna go and make it happen. Why? Because I've decided so".

A moment of such attitude and empowering self-talk is so important. That's a moment when you're destiny is shaped. You're constantly choosing. It's all about the micro-decisions you take and your continual emotional awareness. So begin to steer your thoughts towards greatness. Focus on what you'd love to experience.

Am I in my Queen energy or my lower self?
What thoughts am I projecting through my mind?
What emotions am I running through my body?

It's your absolute responsibility to keep the vision alive. If you don't, then who will? No one. It's at this moment, when we least want to do the work, that we must do the work. Your faith will be tested.

It will be given to those who believe and ONLY onto those

In moments when you're faced with a roadblock or a challenge, it's easy to get caught up in the frantic hustle and day-to-day grind. To blindly dive in to work without clarifying your vision or desired outcomes. Often the basic problem lies in being disconnected from your soul and your most exciting vision. So, you're either running around out of control or, on another extreme, completely avoiding taking action at all costs.

QUEEN RULE#

Plan your day in a way that something definite must be accomplished towards your aim, your ambition. Set 1 big and 2 smaller outcomes for your day, week and a month.

MY 3 TOP INTENTIONS FOR TODAY ARE:
MY TOP 3 INTENTIONS FOR THIS WEEK ARE:
MY TOP 3 INTENTIONS FOR THE MONTH ARE:

Let me ask you:

Is this thing you're pursuing now actually aligned to what I deeply want? Are you focused on getting the outcomes Y-O-U desire?

To provide you with a better understanding, here's an example from my own life:

I used to live in and run my business from London. What I supposedly wanted was to create significantly much more money and be able to move out to a bigger apartment in a better area. Or so I thought. I made myself work obsessively over setting new business structures, spent countless nights studying internet marketing and doing whatever I knew to bring in more money. Yet, my soul somehow wasn't in it. Things weren't working out. The more I pushed for it, the more I was pushed away from it. The whole experience seemed draining and I made myself miserable though the process. I neglected my diet, my time outdoors, time out with my friends and my self-care.

At some point, something deep within made me take my journal, sit on a terrace and ask the questions I missed…

*"Justina, honestly, what is that you really, really, really want?
What's the life you desire to create for yourself?
What's the purpose of moving out to a bigger apartment"*

I allowed the answers to flow and teared up in solitude. The truth was I didn't even want a bigger apartment in London. Actually, I didn't even want to live in London! WOW! That was a huge wake-up call for me.

Over time, I realised it was my ego's wishes and not my soul's desire. Yes, my soul craved a different lifestyle experience… what I desired from the bottom of my feminine soul was to move out, to Spain, not London!!! After a few months, I decided to spend a season in Mallorca, rented a bigger apartment for myself, made the money I needed in the meantime and even wrote my first book, *"The Rich Soul"*.

So my teaching point for you here is this:

GO FOR WHAT YOUR SOUL CRAVES, NOT WHAT YOUR EGO DEMANDS

By this time, you've learned that there's no need to jump into fantasy land and cut yourself short. While setting a new exciting vision for yourself, what matters the most is that you're completely aligned with your spiritual source. In order to support you in that, I've got for you some helpful exercises:

- What business goals, projects, trips, experiences or relationships does your soul crave to achieve next?

OPPORTUNITY TO JOURNAL

Go inside and wait for the truth. Dig deep and answer in writing in as much detail as possible! Every time you come up with an answer, keep asking "why?" Connect your answers to feelings and emotions, not just facts, to make them more compelling. Try to avoid turning this into a boring 'to-do list' writing session. Think big picture dreams!

1. If you had no limiting beliefs, what would you want for your life? What about your business?
2. What legacy do you want to have? Why?
3. What do you want to be known for? Why?
4. What kind of lifestyle do you want, in detail? Why?
5. What are you not willing to compromise on? Why?
6. What would you regret NOT doing, having, or being at the end of the year? How about at the end of your life?
7. What do you want to accomplish in the next 6 months? Year? 5 years? Why?
8. Who do you want to become?

QUEEN WALK EXERCISE:

I'll share a favourite practice I learned. It's called the Queen Walk and I frequently recommend it to my clients. The directions are simple:

Take a walk for no shorter than 20 minutes and as you do so, place a hand on your heart and silently repeat to yourself "I am the Queen" every time your eyes light on an object - a crack in the sidewalk, a blade of grass, a face, a cloud, a car, etc. This practice is profound. It helps you instantaneously reclaim your dignity, majesty, and rulership — without vanity.

Chapter Five

QUEENS CONTROL THEIR EMOTIONS

"We need women who are so strong they can be gentle, so educated they can be humble, so fierce they can be compassionate, so passionate they can be rational and so disciplined they can be free"
— ANONYMOUS

Throughout history, women have traditionally been viewed as driven by their emotions rather than rational thinking. And rightly so. As women, our nervous system is wired to firstly FEEL and then THINK, unlike men to men. We've always been perceived as fairer, delicate, emotional and sensitive. Our feminine essence deep within quickly attends to the emotional needs of a newborn baby, our loved ones and is touch with its sensitive Heart.

Yet, are we supposed to continue justifying our tantrums, hysteria, the attacks of blame and lack of self-control with this logic? I believe at this point in our growth, we can do way much better than this. Please don't get me wrong: I'm not suggesting you repress your emotions at all costs, deny them or diminish their importance. That would be foolish and immature. What I propose in this chapter is that you gaining a wider perspective and self-control about the way how you choose to manage your emotions the moment you're triggered.

As spiritually evolved women, we must develop a self-mastery around the domain of our emotions. Without emotional self-control, we risk harming or destroying our invaluable reputation, finances or relationships. As you can see, the stakes are way too high to be overlooked.

The Queen and her realm won't survive
without a reliable reputation

It's so frequent in our daily lives that we deal with situations that provoke a strong emotional reaction. Not always are we are stable enough to cope with what life puts on our shoulders: your child may get sick, an argument with your partner ore ven the death of a relative might hit you.

The truth is our instinctive behaviour is dictated by our unmet emotional needs. As a result, we threat, despair, withdraw or run away. This is why we fall prey to our impulsive emotional reactions. Helpless, we don't know any better. Yet, there's a new way. A way of the Queen.

Queens Rule:
A QUEEN DEMONSTRATES HER MENTAL
AND EMOCIONAL SANITY

Queens have mastered *the art of not panicking*. She won't explode, furious, crying or shouting in rage in public. Instead, she is able to keep her cool, in touch with her emotions, yet not let them overpower her and escalate too quickly.

The reason? A woman who can't demonstrate she's able to keep her emotions under control won't be trusted with power and responsibility.

We must learn how to develop emotionally and be mature enough to be able to self-regulate and take a stand for our needs without unnecessary dramas. So many of our mistakes and regretful behaviours stem from the fact we let our emotions take control over us.

"The journey has to feel you want the destination to feel"
—DANIELLE LA PORTE

As the Queen that you're becoming, your reputation and inner strength are directly related to the level you feel your emotions and are able to do what's right.

I've seen many women throwing tantrums, giving up in desperation or be unable to control their emotions. Consequences? They lost their money, harmed their relationships or regretted their behaviour with the children.

The lesson from this chapter is that you can be the master of your emotions — not their victim.

THE RULES CAN CHANGE

If, in your childhood, you had to adopt 'unhealthy' coping mechanisms to survive because of your family dynamics (like alcoholism, domestic violence, death of a parent etc), or traumas you've been through, know that you can unlearn them and teach yourself a different way.

Investigate. Journal. Seek help. Voice out loud what you feel with your best friend. What did you feel back then when you got triggered. As you're healing, let your own intuition guide you where to place your focus.

For example, you might start getting the message that it's time to transform your relationship dynamics. That doesn't necessarily mean: *"Ok, my intuition tells me I'm so unhappy with him now that tomorrow I'll break up or ask for a divorce"*. If you rush into things impulsively, you may not be prepared and grounded enough to move on with changes. Trust your instincts but keep your feet well on the ground. Our visions and instincts are simply the starting points. It's our responsibility to keep checking in internally and keep adjusting, keep asking:

What's in service of my soul's growth in this situation?

You may well get a different answer as to how unsatisfied emotional needs can be met ...and you would never have needed to say anything in haste out loud to your partner.

Take responsibility for your own satisfaction and wellbeing by establishing clear conditions that work for you and are fair for both.

There's a chance that, with just a little tweak, you'll achieve a great improvement in your relationship and spare yourself the breakup.

MAKE DECISIONS WITH A CLEAR MIND

You're no longer the same person you once were. You're no longer the defenseless child at the mercy of your parents. You're an adult woman, who has to reclaim the responsibility for her greatest destiny.

You've levelled up, you've grown up, you've transformed and are doing the work required to treat those unhealed parts of you. To get back in touch with the reality of the situation, instead of a childlike idealisation.

When this happens, it's very easy to get carried away and quickly fall into extremes. It could make you react impulsively to situations, adopt an *"all or nothing"* attitude to now make up for lost time when there's no real need to do so.

What I suggest is that you give yourself more time. What if you allowed the impulse of the moment to pass and then think with a clear mind? I know it requires moment to moment awareness but firstly try anchoring yourself with a deep breath and just be. Delaying the reaction will give you time to ponder the consequences and alternatives. And that's important when there's a chance that the behaviour you considered right in the moment, may actually cause you stress and remorse.

Be certain you are comfortable with what you're doing. This way, you won't be consumed by the guilt afterward of *" I wished I hadn´t acted so impulsively"*.

SLOW DOWN

Give yourself the time to act… or not to act out. What do you regret most often about the things you do too quickly? My clients usually regret their offensive words, overreacting or spending money without considering the consequences.

If you're not receiving some professional help in this area, here are ways you can begin to overcome impulsivity.

Begin by taking a look at the other people it may impact upon. Ask yourself and notice:

Who else is going to be affected by this behaviour?

How are they going to be affected by what I do?
Then move to reconnect with your soul and a higher perspective. Here, I like to ask my clients questions like:

Where's Your Truth?
What does your heart yearn for?
For Whom?

Such questions put you in charge of your reactions, to understand them. What a very special place to be because ultimately, your behaviour has consequences.

Ask yourself: *Is it worth it?* If so, then enjoy the experience. If it's not, be disciplined enough to let go of it.

For example, you might impulsively feel: *"I want to file for a divorce, I can't stand it anymore"*. Is it worth it? Is the divorce really what you want in this situation? Or maybe what you actually want is simply different dynamics with your partner, where you both have your needs met in a new way. Perhaps a respectful communication, being heard and seen is what you truly yearn for deep within and you're just not expressing it.

Another example is that you might feel tempted to satisfy an emotional frustration with sweets or extra sugar craving as some sort of comfort. Is it worth it? Is this impulse worth ruining your blood levels and all the diet efforts you've been making for the last few weeks? Won't you regret it afterward? If you won't, go ahead and enjoy the experience. But if you'd rather see yourself looking sexy in the mirror in your new dress, put it down and resist this impulse.

My teaching point here: Your feminine power lies in your self-control, having the presence of mind to make great decisions for yourself in the moment.

BEING MANIPULATED VC HAVING SELF-CONTROL

Being manipulated entails living in ever-lasting emotional drama and functioning as a hysterical victim of your circumstances or menstrual cycle, while at the same time everyone around you has great fun pushing all your buttons and playing you like a fool. They used to confuse your kindness with weakness. Luckily, that game is OVER. Us Queens, we know how to keep it cool. Your emotions are here to guide you, not ruin your life or your finances.

There's no need for emotional drama. There's no need to add more suffering to an already challenging situation in your life. Instead, understand that your feelings aren't random, they're messengers. Let them speak to you and guide you towards the underlying truth.

Here's how you can listen to your emotions and understand the message for you:

- Bitterness shows you where you need to heal, where you're still holding judgments on others and yourself.

- Resentment shows you where you're living in the past and not allowing the present to be as you want it.

- Discomfort shows you that you need to pay attention right now to what's happening because you're being given the opportunity to change, to shift the course of your life and not repeat your default pattern.

- Anger shows you what you're passionate about, where your boundaries are, what obstacles you must destroy and what you believe must be transformed around you.

- Guilt shows you that you're still living a life based on other people's expectations of what you should do.

- Shame shows you that you're internalising other people's beliefs about who you should be and that you need to reconnect with yourself…take pride in just being you.

- Anxiety shows you that you need to anchor yourself in the here and now. You're living in fear of the future, scaring yourself with your imagination.

- Sadness shows you the depth of your feeling, the depth of your care for others and this world, it invites you to simply be grateful for what you have been given and teaches you to detach and to let go

Make more space to consider the emotion that keeps showing up for you most often. What's the message this emotion keeps bringing up for you?

In order to get more clarity, try a third-person perspective: Look at yourself as if you were standing by your side. Observe that person. Feel her needs and longings. Feel. What is that person needing the most now?

Queen Rule: **Queens are unavailable for drama.**

BEGIN TO SET PERSONAL BOUNDARIES

Countries establish physical boundaries to protect their territories. People have formal and emotional boundaries to protect their sanity and resources. Setting boundaries however, is challenging for *most* people. It's especially tough for women who are too kind and have been infected with a *"disease to please"*.

A healthy boundary protects you from being exhausted, overwhelmed and frustrated. It acts as a rule to set the clear conditions that serve and empower you from those that don't.

Setting boundaries is a big leap towards self-respect

At some point in your life, you'll be forced to set healthy boundaries in order to protect your wellbeing. I admit, setting boundaries might feel like the most hard-core inner work that you've ever been forced to do. I remember how being able to say *"I'm sorry, I can't lend you more money"* to one of my best friends, tested my ability to say "no". Yet, every "NO" you say because of your healthy boundaries, is a sacred "YES" to yourself.

So begin setting simple but firm boundaries with a graceful or neutral tone. Setting healthy boundaries takes some real-life experience and practice. Take a look at the examples below to get an idea:

In order to protect your time, energy and resources it's OK for you to:

A. Prioritise your needs
B. Stop giving too much out of need or desperation
C. Use simple, direct language
D. Set clear and precise conditions with others
E. Say "NO" to extra, unexpected demands
F. To back out of the commitment
G. Have people accept legally written statements of your professional boundaries

Examples:

- **Prioritise your needs** – You are allowed to get in touch with your needs first and set clear terms of what they are before you engage in any activity, deal or collaboration.

BOUNDARY FIX: Ask yourself: *"What's in it for me? Under what conditions would this work well for me?"* Then voice out loud your terms and conditions, seeking a fair dynamics.

- **Stop overgiving out of desperation** – Are you the one who just gives and gives but receives very little or nothing for it? There's no need for you to overcompensate for anything. Find a fair balance. Don't seek control by overgiving. Seek what's fair and reasonable by setting your expectations clearly. People don't love you because you give them more. Allow yourself to be loved because of who you are. Get clarity beforehand about the value you're exchanging with others. Specify the terms, the time, the financial costs. Don't expect others to read your mind. Speak yours out loud and protect your own business without emotional co-dependency.

BOUNDARY FIX: Say: *"What do I expect in return? What would make me satisfied on my side?* and then, *"what I find fair for me and what I would expect… XYZ. What's your opinion?"*

WOUNDED WOMAN	AWAKENED WOMAN
Tolerates harmful behaviours	Sets loving boundaries
Afraid to speak her truth	Honours her truth
Lacks self-worth	Claims her worth
Seeks external validation	Validated from within
People pleases	Inspires others to shine
Apologises for who she is	Lives unapologetically
Has negative self-talk	Speaks gently to herself

QUEENS TURN PAIN INTO POWER

You are going to make it through this season.
You are going to see the other side of this.
You are going to find peace in the confusion of all that does not make sense now

A woman who is alert and awake doesn't wait for a disaster to get the message. Sadly, sometimes our previous conditioning has left us so out of touch with our true selves that we only finally get the message about something that should have been obvious, once we've got ourselves into a huge mess. We've all been hurt and isolated. We had to nurse our wounds in solitude.

This is when a Queen takes her time. And then she takes a clear stand. She becomes her own rescue and decides it's time to do whatever takes, to make that full commitment upfront.

Whether it's YES or NO, a Queen has the courage to confront even a seemingly impossible situation and clearly confront it.

At this part of your journey, it's time for you learn how to turn pain into power.

SHADOW EXERCISE:

Here's an exercise I learned from my mentor Gina DeVee, that helped me to transform my pain into power.

Shadows overtake us in fear.

In the table below write down your 1 specific shadow of your disempowered self, disempowered way of operating in the world, mostly unconsciously.

I have given some examples. Name your shadow. Get intuitive and creative.

Then, next to it, write the transformed, enlightened version of that shadow. Once you do it, think about what desire is hiding behind the shadow and also being empowered by its transformation.

SHADOW	SHADOW TRANSFORMED	DESIRE
My Cinderella - self	Queen of Greatness	To live in a beautiful house and look glamorous
Deprived of joy in business	Queen of Joy in Business	To hit 6 figures in my business
Miss *"Never Enough"*	Queen of Making Money	To release any past debt and accumulate £30.000 in savings
Unloved Little Girl	Queen of Love	To create a conscious and loving relationship with my spiritual partner / husband

TIME TO JOURNAL:

1. What does the healthy version of you look like in that área once your shadow is removed?

2. What elements are necessary in order to bring that desire to fruition?

3. What caused the shadow, what was I trying to disown?

4. What aspect of my life do I need to take full ownership of?

5. Practice a creative visualisation of you ideal outcome and situation in that area. Write down your precise vision.

PART II

Stepping Towards Your New Destiny as a Queen

Chapter Six

QUEENS EXUDE REGAL PRESENCE

"Let others see their own greatness when looking in your eyes."
— MOLLIE MARTI

You know that woman who walks into the room, impresses everyone from the very first moment, delivers a message and everyone's eyes are glued to her, listening to every word?

She commands attention and respect from the moment she appears — not because of the volume of her voice, but the wisdom and confidence behind it. She owns the room with unassuming boldness. Everyone appreciates the glow of her feminine radiance. There is something about her demeanour that dominates the space she's in. Something about her presence announces that a Queen has stepped into the room.

A woman who represents the most prominent example of such a powerful presence was Princess Diana (you'll realise by now how much of an influence she has had no me!). Her presence made the environment brighter. She was able to enchant her audience since the moment she appeared, gracefully show up for her public duties, use her position to help others and take a bold stand as a feminine leader.

This woman has what is called a regal presence. This woman will be YOU.

A QUEEN SPEAKS BEFORE SHE OPENS HER MOUTH

When a Queen speaks, everyone is eager to listen. Her words carry pearls of wisdom. What a contrast that is to the communication expressed by those still blind to what they could be. Instead of powerful words that inspire and elevate others, you'll hear trash, meaningless conversations, rumours, swearing, blaming and words of discontent.

BE THE EXCEPTION
Be The Gracious, Loving, Fierce, Fair, Capable, Wise Woman with a beautiful spirit and a receiving heart.

We live in times when so many women feel emotionally drained and abandoned, begging for even a tiny sign of attention and affection. We lose our emotional stability and, sense of dignity, instead, falling prey to our desperate reactions.

The immature parts within us make us desperately chase for approval and validation from others. They make us shrink, sacrifice and doubt ourselves. They make us lose our feminine presence. I used to be that woman too. And I know how devastating this *desperate mode* is.

If my Heart could speak words in those moments she would say:

This is not You, Sweetheart — this is an impostor. Show it to the door.

On your journey, your false beliefs and judgments will be constantly brought to the surface for you to look at them through experiences that can hit your heart hard.

Let's press a RESET button. Let's do it over and do it better now.

A QUEEN ALWAYS RISES ABOVE THE STANDARD AND RESETS THE BAR

True Queens never need to fight for attention because they possess the gift of presence. When a woman reconnects with that presence, her whole life is transformed. She becomes more attractive, grounded, and sensual.

WHAT IS PRESENCE THEN?

Presence is about authentic excellence and class. It goes way deeper than just the mere physical existence in time and space.

A Queen's presence is the internal energy she emanates. Her aura. The core of her essence. The combination of her gestures, looks, and demeanour. The presence emanating from the soul of the Queen is noble. Such a woman is characterised by her ambition, work ethic, spiritual maturity, and leadership skills.

She's pure on the inside. At all times, powered from within. Such a woman is self-assured, not in a need for outside validation. She is sure of herself and her worth, responding to her environment, with grace and humility.

DEVELOP YOUR FEMININE PRESENCE

Do you desire to attract the attention you want? I thought so! I will be sharing with you the best practices to develop that magnetic quality that gets you noticed.

The feminine energy in your body concentrates around your hip area and lower belly ascending to the heart. To be more specific, the 'presence' centre for a woman lies in the area 3 inches right below your belly button. Whereas, the masculine energy gathers around torso and the upper chest and arms.

Have you ever observed that when you're stressed and tired, your energy goes up to that upper body area? I'm talking about the times when your attention loses focus, you're just spinning mentally in your head, absorbed by so many external things that you need to take care of. You tense your arms, get excessively stressed and at the same time lose touch with your body and the access to your intuition. What happens to your presence in these moments?

When our attention is OUTSIDE of our body our feminine presence vanishes

When our attention is INSIDE our body our feminine presence reappears

BEST PRACTICE TO INCREASE YOUR ENERGETICAL PRESENCE:

- **Hone your energetic power as a woman.** Before you walk into a room or are about to communicate an important message, consciously bring your attention to that power point, 3 inches below your belly button. Focus on your womb space and place your attention in that area. Connect with your hips. Breath to that area. Then, once connected, speak from that place allowing it to flow with feminine grace. From there, people will relate to you differently and much more profoundly. Trust me, your audience will feel a big difference.

PHYSICAL PRESENCE:

1. **When standing, check your posture**. Be grounded in your body. Own your curves. Bring your shoulders back and hold your head high. Imagine the top of your head being pulled up to the sky, elongating your spine.

2. When sitting, take up space. If you've been invited to the table, you belong there. Don't wrap yourself in a ball with hunched shoulders, crossed arms and legs. Put both feet on the floor, open your chest. This allows your breath to flow more fully and your voice to sound more confident.

3. When meeting someone, look them directly in the eyes. This conveys self-assurance.

ESTABLISH YOUR UNIQUE VOICE:

When I was growing up, I remember being "shushed" and silenced a lot. Does that sound familiar? I was told I talked too much or at the wrong time, such as when my parents needed rest. For a long time I made it mean no one wanted to listen to me, so what's the point in using my voice. Having an opinion used to get me in trouble, so from an early age, I started to censor myself. Instead, I began being an avid writer and journaler.

I hid my true self for decades. I constantly put others first (saying no to myself) in order to keep people. I limited what I could do, renouncing my right to stand up for myself. I passively put up with the way things were.

We don't need to sound like men to be heard. Instead, we need to give ourselves permission to express our voice in a way that conveys the truth of our heart:

A. **Watch the language you use.** Make sure your words express the level of your education and personal culture. I'd suggest you get rid of public verbal vulgarity. Words have consequences and the price is your reputation. Be an example. Be an exception. Can't you find more educated words to communicate with? In addition, lose the *"I'm struggling... I'm so sorry..."* Pay attention to how many times you apologise and ask yourself whether an apology is really necessary, or if it's an excessive habit you perpetuate from need or fear of upsetting others to be excessively kind and have to break.

B. **Eliminate the doubt when delivering a message.** Instead of starting off with, *"Maybe we can try it this way..."* shift to, *"I recommend this approach."* You will notice that your words have more impact!

C. **Practice, practice and more practice.** Not in your head, but out loud. Practice in the mirror and ask for feedback from people you trust. You'll be amazed at the difference it makes.

Your personal presence is your power. Your impact. Your confidence. That power is within you and you can access it anytime. All you have to do is to set an intention: *"I reclaim all my power now. I am beautifully present. I choose to shine fully with my light."*.

Make deliberate use of your presence for the good of others who come into contact with you. Delight. Enchant. Grace them. Open your mouth to bless, heal and inspire others. Present yourself publicly with pride and self-appreciation. So next time you go out, drop your shoulders back and lift your chin up. Practice carrying yourself with class. Don't be available for self-depreciation or feeling small.

PRESENCE: UNCONDITIONAL SELF-LOVE

Self-love is so important. Because when you're all alone and it's 3 in the morning and you're lying on the floor crying and shaking and wishing it all would end, who's going to be there for you? YOU. You have to pick yourself up and find the strength to carry on. At the end of the day, you're all you've got.

On my journey, I observed that my personal presence grew in those times when I felt the vibration of unconditional love towards myself. Let me explain. The self-help world encourages us to practice self-love. Tell yourself sweet words and treat yourself nicely. That's great. But who loves you when you get angry when you're afraid? How about the times when all you want to do is beat yourself up over the way you look or figure out that again, you haven't given your all?

Well, that person needs to be you. You deserve and need your own unconditional love.

Basic self-love in those moments wasn't enough for me. I needed more. I needed a radical, deep and profound, unconditional love. I needed to own the understanding that I am the source of my reality. I needed to open my heart in moments when I most wanted to shut it down: when a friend told a truth that hurt me when I got rejected, criticised and left alone. To me, that's a hardcore spiritual practice.

I went back to basics. I grabbed a mirror and would get present first of all with my own soul. I looked into my eyes and said out loud: *"Justina, I do, I love you unconditionally"*.

And I would repeat this to myself a good 20 times. While doing it for the first time, I would just burst into tears. If the same happens to you with this exercise, allow the emotions to flow through you. The feeling is healing. With more repetitions, I sensed a deeper connection and a new level of self-acceptance. I recommend you start offering yourself that depth of articulated unconditional love, too. It's soul-soothing.

Before we finish this chapter, I want to share one more practice that empowered me tremendously. I learned this particular practice from an incredible woman whom I admire dearly. She's a real Queen of her life. Her name is Lisa Nichols, an American motivational speaker.

In one of her speeches she shared a practice that lifted her up in times when life had got her on her knees and she needed to find the strength to face her challenges:

Lisa recommends practicing with the 3 statements below. Insert your name and work through them, one by one. I used to journal them, but feel free to get present with them either in the shower or in front of your bathroom mirror. It goes like this:

- **Justina, I am proud of you for:**

The intention of this statement is to celebrate yourself. We're taught to not take too much pride in ourselves and brush off our merits. We're undervalued. But we need that winning feeling to get into our momentum. To feel great about ourselves and strongly grounded in what we're capable of making happen.

Then, list or say 7 things you are proud of about yourself. From the tiniest thing such as putting on great makeup, a random act of kindness, to earning x amount of money. It all counts.

1.
2.
3.
4.
5.
6.
7

Next, you'll practice releasing and self-forgiveness. Our hurtful thoughts want to invade us constantly. I found release when doing this. Often my eyes would fill with a river of tears, but then… I could breathe lighter. I would stand up taller. I want the same for you.

- **Justina, I forgive you for:**

1.
2.
3.
4.
5.
6.
7

Lastly, self- commitment. We're so quick to commit to other people's agenda and lose sight of what works best for us. I used this last statement to recommit to what my soul asked of me. Then, during the day I was mindful to stay true to what I promised myself in the morning. It worked wonders!

- **Justina, I commit to you that:**

1.
2.
3.
4.
5.
6.
7

What does deepening into your feminine presence would look like to you? What would you start doing more of? What would you stop doing?

Chapter Seven

QUEENS RESPECTFULLY CLAIM THEIR WORTH

"Until you value yourself, you won't value your time. Until you value your time, you will not do anything with it."

— M. SCOTT PECK, THE ROAD LESS TRAVELLED

WHEN YOU DON'T FEEL WORTHY

So many of us hold a deep belief that we were born unworthy. In our culture, we suffer emotionally and mentally from an epidemic of unworthiness. The wound runs deep.

As spiritually evolved women, we've given ourselves way too much room to still question our own worthiness at every step along the way. We're afraid to bet on ourselves 100%. We're concerned whether we can actually accomplish the goal we'd like to set. The inner dialogue inside our head repeats the question *"Am I good enough…?"* For that man. For those clients. For this amount of money. For such a body. For such a house. For such a life. We get paralysed by the question. We hold ourselves back, comparing and waiting for outside validation in order to make the leap.

That level of diminishing yourself and small-minded thinking reflects a still immature part of us, still standing in our way. We've got to heal that part lovingly and reclaim a true sense of our worth.

So I've got to tell you… such conversation so last decade! It's so NOT you. Looking at what you stand for, how much you've overcome in your life, how much value you provide for others, and ultimately, at what gifts you've been given by God… now it's high time to finally repair what has been broken. That is, the deep knowing, that profound conviction of how much you mean to this world and how valuable you are to all of us. It's time to rediscover what a treasure you are to others and also, how much you should treasure yourself

Are you open and willing to own this process step by step and begin to live out that truth in your life?

As the child of an alcoholic parent, reestablishing my own sense of self-worth was a huge lesson for me. I've always considered myself a pretty sociable, smart and daring girl. *"Me and low self-worth? Are you kidding me?"* Yet my relationship dynamics, client interactions or financial choices showed me otherwise. I had to face this issue head-on and address the core of my deepest suffering, the sense of *'not enough'*. So one day, I admitted to myself in my journal *"You know what, Justina? I really want to value you at a much higher level. You're a Superstar and I know it. But there's something within me that's is terrified to admit it."* That morning I got in touch with an immature part of me that felt completely worthless…realising this left me deeply shaken

Me?! A successful woman, attractive, intelligent, spoke 4 languages, travelled around the world, full of passion for her purpose of elevating the consciousness of females around the globe! Yes. That same woman, deep within still carried a shy and desperate Little Girl who at times still felt a sense of shame and worthlessness.

During the first moments, I was embarrassed to recognise it. I teared up. After a while, my soul empowered me to take radical responsibility for that wounded part of me. The key word in that moment was: *gentle.* We need to give ourselves a gentle healing space and respect our subconscious defense mechanisms. It created such a way of being in order to protect us and guarantee our survival, even though it may seem counter-productive. My sense of unworthiness in the world had prevented me from reaching my full potential, taking pride in myself and being seen as the real me, all to avoid rejection, criticism or ridicule.

These days, if old thoughts of self-doubt or unworthiness occur to me and I notice feeling like taking a backward step out of fear… I say to myself *"Real Justina, please come forth now!"*. I do it intentionally, to make contact again with the healthiest parts of my personality and make my decisions and actions from that place. It always gives me the courage to take bolder actions!

FEEL YOUR WORTH

You've always been beautiful and valuable. Now you're just deciding to be wiser, faster, stronger, fitter, bolder. Keep that perspective.

The mistake we make in how we perceive our true value is that we look for confirmation of it from others. It goes like this:

- *"If he chooses me and loves me, that proves me I'm valuable and worthy of love."*
- *If that client hires me and pays me this rate, I will know I'm worthy enough to charge at this level.*
- *If my boss acknowledges my work and dedication, I will know I'm worthy of a promotion. etc".*

Yet, it doesn't work this way. We can't expect from others, what we aren't willing to do for ourselves, and that is to first truly believe in our value. It doesn't come from other people's opinions of you. Nor does it come from their approval of what you do, or whether or not they say yes or no to you. I love how Brene Brown, An American author and speaker puts it: *"If you're not in the arena also getting your ass kicked, I'm not interested in your feedback.* Boom! Take that in.

What people give or do not give you, say or don't say to you must not stop you expressing your purpose. Instead, you must be so deeply rooted in the truth about your own value, how glorious and capable you are that NOTHING, absolutely nothing can stop you or take you out of the game.

Your value as a woman is not determined by your current bank account statements, by your weight, by a man by your side or the way you look. It comes straight from God. Yet, so many times we wish from other others, the very thing that only God can do for us. To ground us in our value and our purpose. I repeat: Your value comes from God. You're unconditionally worthy.

"My value comes from God.
Your approval or disapproval means nothing to me"

Too often, we consider ourselves inappropriate for our tasks assigned by God. *Who?? Me? No way!* The Bible shows us examples such as Queen Esther, a Jewish orphaned girl who was called in to become the Queen of Persia. She had to accept with dignity her divine calling and surrender herself to the God plan. God has a great plan for your Life.

God loves you and he can do anything, even with your broken pieces. Walk by faith, not by fear. Say aloud to the universe:

"I know I AM your chosen one, God.
I humbly accept my divine calling. I receive your blessing, God.
I see now how I fit in the world and how valuable I am and how much the world needs me. I thank you for your ever-present gui-
dance on my path."

It's imperative, that as the Queen that you are, you quit relying on other people to confirm your value. You don't need their approval to feel good about yourself. You don't need their encouragement to feel good about yourself. What you do need in those moments is you being there for you: encouraging, approving, making yourself feel good about what you're up to.

So pay attention to your behaviours, like always second-guessing yourself, always being dependent on checking in with others about what you should do next. I don't mean having a wider perspective through the views of others is wrong. What I mean is that others can't possibly know what's best for you, your desires and your soul's growth. What's required at this stage, is that you get so connected with you and your unique value in the world, that you find the courage to make that bold decision your soul is begging you for, despite the fear, risk or odds. And then be completely accountable at every step of the way. Keep checking in with yourself: *"How can I take more responsibility for my outcomes in this situation?"*

QUEENS RULE

QUEENS ARE SKILLED AT MAKING BOLD DECISIONS FOR THEMSELVES

"When someone treats you like you're just one of many options, help them narrow their choice by removing yourself from the equation. Sometimes you have to try not to care, no matter how much you do. Because sometimes you can mean almost nothing to someone who means so much to you. It's not pride — it's self-respect. Don't give part-time people a full-time position in your life. Know your value and what you have to offer and never settle for anything less than you desire. "

YOU MUST FIND THE COURAGE TO LEAVE THE TABLE IF RESPECT IS NO LONGER BEING SERVED

Women with a wounded sense of self-worth tend to be excessively loyal — even in the face of evidence that the other party does not deserve it. Instead of seeing the full situation for what it truly is, they keep hoping things will just change. They overstay in a relationship that no longer keeps them growing and satisfying their needs, maintain outdated friendships that provide no value to their lives, just because they have known each other for a long time and keep hoping and wishing for dream clients that only tell them "yes". The cost is their precious resources like drained mental energy by excessive thinking, lost money and worse, the wasted passing of time.

As a Queen, you have honour and respect for your financial, mental and emotional resources — no matter how big or small.

A woman with a healthy sense of self-worth doesn't want ANYONE who doesn't want her. It's far more beneficial to allocate your energy to those things over which you have control: your responsibilities, decisions, and emotions. Being dependent energetically on the reactions of someone else, who may or may not be there for you, puts you in a place that you can't control and you're giving your power away. Don`t do that! Instead, be courageous enough to reallocate your resources to where they're appreciated, valued and well invested for the long-term.

CONTINOUS IMPROVEMENT IS BETTER THAN DELAYED PERFECTION

Another trait of wounded self-worth is a desperate chase for recognition. It stems from a negative self-image formed in childhood. In order to fix it as an adult, such women become perfectionists. They rescue the needy, they are obliging, hard-working, they overly sacrifice and devote themselves to others — but in return, they expect gratitude and friendship and love.

Without a healthy instinct around your self-worth you may:

- **excessively sacrifice or give** in order to receive signs of love, approval or validation, and ultimately prove you're *"worthy enough"*

- **become emotionally attached and extremely loyal**, justifying unreciprocated behaviour, pointlessly waiting, not setting up clear exit terms so that you don't end up wasting your resources

- **refuse to see the whole picture** with regards to a problematic situation, omitting the important yet unpleasant parts that if accepted may initially hurt, but would make take full responsibility for the outcome

INSECURITY AND ROYALTY WILL NEVER COEXIST

You weren't born insecure. That's not your real character. You were trained and conditioned to behave like an insecure person. You've been indoctrinated with lies limiting you. You've been taught to never blow your own trumpet but to think about yourself way below the level of the Queenly, shining Superstar that you are.

However, the true voice within you, the voice of your Queen says: *I am capable. I can make it happen. I am a woman who can carry more power — in my life, with my money, with my contribution to the world.*

Insecurity is a mental attitude that forces us to operate below our potential due to fear and shame

Negativity and self-doubt never go hand in hand with power and prosperity. Such a mindset must be eradicated forcefully from your consciousness. As fear, insecurity and self-doubt never leave your mind willingly (they feed off your energy), you must shut that mental space. You must manage your mind and redirect it from things that don't matter. Say NO. Say STOP.

Your low self-worth and insecurities may be due to having an experience of your body being shamed or criticised. I'm so sorry. I have so much compassion for you. But now, your healing will consist of teaching yourself how to have pride in your body. What it takes is for you look in the mirror and falling in love with exactly that what God has given you. I want you to be assured of is that despite any possibly harsh judgements about your size and shape, there is a wise, loving man out there who dreams exactly about what you represent.

CLAIM YOUR FINANCIAL SECURITY

Queens are very good at managing their finances. They've learned how to be financially astute, prudent and resourceful. Most importantly, they've learned how to stand firmly on their own two feet.

Undoubtedly, times have changed, a lot. I am a great advocate for receiving graciously, especially from men. I absolutely appreciate the masculine protection and provision. However, I am an even greater advocate for depending absolutely on myself for my financial well-being. Yet, most women are not prepared to financially thrive on their own. Too often, they may not even realise just how dependent they are until faced with a personal 'wake-up call' or crisis.

One woman, whom I consider a Queen of making money, is the famous investor, Kim Kiyosaki. She points out that our self-esteem is highly linked to our ability to provide for ourselves and is an excellent example of how empowered women have a healthy relationship with making, managing and multiplying money.

The statistics about women and money are startling . In the US:

- 47 percent of women over the age of 50 are single
- Women have a lower retirement income because they are away from work 14.7 years on average, compared to 1.6 years for men
- 50 percent of marriages end in divorce (and women usually end up with the kids)
- After divorce, a woman's standard of living drops an average of 73%
- As of 2000, women are expected to live an average of 7 to 10 years longer than men
- The average woman born between 1948 and 1964 may likely remain in the workforce until at least 74 years of age due to inadequate savings and pension coverage
- 3 out of 4 elderly living in poverty are women (80 percent were not poor when their husbands were alive)
- 90 percent of women will have sole responsibility for their finances within their lifetime, yet 79 percent have not planned for this
- 58 percent of female baby boomers have less than $10,000 in retirement

These numbers point out something absolutely key. You must value having money over just spending it or giving it away too quickly to others. You must make sure you're financially supported, protected and provided for. So your task is to be as financially intelligent as you are beautiful. Value having money. Appreciate it and use your resources wisely.

The Queen Golden Rule: #
SHE WHO HAS THE GOLD, MAKES THE RULES.

Journalling time:

EXERCISES — Look deeper at your beliefs about your worth:

1. What kind of Queen are you? What is your self-image and self- talk? Is it empowering?

2. Do you take pride in who you are becoming? If so, how? If not, why not?

    a) In order to value myself more, I would have to change my thinking by:

b) In order to value myself more, I would have to act differently by:

Chapter Eight

QUEENS DRESS TO PROJECT POWER

Sweatpants are a sign of defeat.
You lost control of your life so you bought some sweatpants.
— KARL LAGERFELD

A Queen is a woman of intentional. As the position of Queen is powerful, it demands a high level of responsibility. Thus, Queens are purposeful, especially about the way they dress.

GRACE THEM WITH YOUR BEAUTY

We all communicate. Everything you do makes some kind of statement and clothes make a strong visual one about how you feel about yourself. Appropriate dress code is also a way of showing respect for the situation and the other people in it. It has been proven that people are more likely to give money or information to someone if that person is considered well dressed.

I always say that you don't need to show a lot of skin to look alluring. Sensual doesn't mean vulgar. Chic doesn't mean expensive. The French school of female elegance suggests it shall be anything but ostentatious. It's all in the art of suggestion. As Sophia Loren once said, *"Sex appeal is fifty percent what you've got and fifty percent what people think you've got."*

From your hair to your nails, grooming is something that is often overlooked, but nonetheless important. Prioritising grooming can actually cut down prep time and elevates your overall appearance. Everything from functional hairstyles, low maintenance nails to healthy-looking skin can send a message of attention to detail and self-respect.

Remember that empowerment comes from within. Therefore, you should pay close attention to what is happening internally as well as externally and let your clothes reflect the new you. Avoid dramatic looks and work towards enhancing your natural features with soft and subtle techniques.

A Queen demands attention. She evokes the "WOW" factor with her audience through the way she presents herself to the world. She wants to be noticed and seen 'through the crowd.'

A QUEEN RESETS THE BAR AND SET IT HIGHER

When you think of powerful iconic women such as Carolina Herrera, Byron Katie, Beyonce or Oprah Winfrey, one thing they all share in common is a distinctive style. There's a reason some women never change their hair! So whether it's your unique choice of colour, silhouette or pants suit, adopting a signature look will help you to develop a recognisable and visual identity that can communicate reliability.

Class is more than talking politely. It's something about you. When you see a classy lady, this vibration comes mostly from how she holds herself. Who she believes herself to be. You see, you have to believe that you are a classy woman — then it will show itself to others.

THE POWER OF FEMININE CLOTHING

The right choice of clothing a woman wears influences not only how she feels but also makes a vivid statement about who she is, what she wants, or what she's capable of.

The term power dressing is usually understood as a style of clothing used to emphasize and build position, especially in business and politics. To me, *'power dressing'* simply means that you feel like your most empowered, confident and comfortable self.

When it comes to inner confidence, the right outfit can work as a suit of armour to give you that extra boost you need, not just to look the part, but to feel it too and carry yourself accordingly. The purpose of putting on a killer outfit is to help you feel your absolute best.

What should power dressing look like in practice?

There are many ideas and their implementation can be varied. Some suggest imitating the appearance of men, saying that otherwise a woman will not find herself included in the world of business or politics. According to others, emphasising femininity (even with the help of an outfit in a shade of red), can provide an advantage over men, because it stands out from the crowd. Some will look at power dressing through rigid norms that have previously given good results. Others will approach the topic more creatively, looking for new ways to build a convincing image. Regardless, it's always about the interaction between a woman, how the clothes she wears makes her feel and her surroundings in the professional sphere.

Let's take a look at colours. Navy blue is considered a colour which evokes associations with professionalism and authority. Gray is associated with solidity. Black, according to some studies, is treated as a colour of power and firmness. These three colours, so often chosen by men, were quickly adopted by women working in business.

Styles also have similar justifications. We automatically perceive a clear and straight line of extended arms as a sign of strength, firmness and confidence. Appropriate lapels give the silhouette dynamism. A shirt or blouse that covers the neckline, at the same time guarantees that no one will look into this neckline instead of looking at the woman's face. In many cases, the goal of women putting on masculinised attire was to reduce erotic associations in professional situations.

<u>Queens Power-Dressing Rules:</u>

1. **If you show legs, cover-up on top.** If you want to show cleavage, cover your legs more. At the end of the day, you don't want to look like you're trying too hard, nor make people doubt your reputation...

2. **Wear a dress that makes you feel like a million dollars.** That doesn't mean you have to spend a fortune on it. Just make sure its texture is good to high-quality and fits you perfectly.

3. **Lace is very classy.** Black is very classy. Little Black dresses are classy. Simplicity is the ultimate sophistication. **BEWARE**: Wear your underwear in the colour of your clothes. Never do a white bra with a black dress. Also, be careful with transparent clothes. Sometimes they reveal the parts we don't want to reveal.

4. **Spray and delay.** As Christian Dior used to say *Ä woman is not fully dressed without a fragrance"*. **TIP:** Once you lay down a scent on your skin, don't rub it. Let it dry on its

own. My recent discoveries are Molecule 01 EDT and Narciso Rodriguez EDP.

5. **Wear red lipstick.** Maintain the balance. Red lipstick or Smoky eyes. Not both. A stunning necklace or beautiful earrings. My favourite shade of red is Dior Rouge 999.

6. **Choose quality jewellery or go without.** Less is more. Wear your beautiful and original pieces of jewellery. If you don't have anything appropriate, it´s better you go without it. Please avoid any tacky or cheap imitations. Opt for your quality basics. Keep yourself fresh and neat at all times.

7. **The Devil lies in the detail.** Remember about mani, pedi, depilation and fresh breath! It´s the full picture that matters. Such details can totally ruin the look and your confidence. You can't look glamorous with ragged nails!

QUEEN CROWN ADJUSTMENT EXCERCISE:

1. Review your wardrobe thoroughly. What pieces are worn out, have holes or stains in them, yet you still keep them? How about low-quality cheap pieces from a second hand or a local market? Is wearing them empowering to you? I suggest you allow yourself a clothing catharsis and throw away the pieces in your wardrobe that no longer fit you, make you happy, or are not suitable for a Queen.
2. Create a Pinterest vision board and start collecting pictures that represent your style and what inspires you. It´s not only a great visualisation exercise but also can teach you a lot about style and putting clothes together in a coherent composition.

3. Grooming: Make mani and pedi your new non-negotiable. Make sure you keep yourself fresh at all times through fragrance, antiperspirant, and sensual, high-quality lingerie. Your inner woman will thank you for a well-fitting bra!

NOT MY JOB	MY JOB
• Fix people	• Save others
• Be liked	• Please everyone
• Hold it together	• Make others comfortable
• Love people	• Be authentic
• Give myself the love I need	• Speak my honest truth
• Take the next step	• Breathe

**YOU ARE REMEMBERED
FOR THE RULES YOU BREAK**

PART III

Living Your Life According To Queen Rules

Chapter Nine

QUEENS HAVE A POWERFUL RELATIONSHIP WITH GOD

God, thank you for my life.
Thank you for reminding me I have an important purpose to fulfill, that only I can. I surrender all forms of doubt, messiness, laziness, and fear. I open up to the truth of your love, power, forgiveness, and opportunities. I desire a deeper connection with you. I desire to cultivate a greater power. I know you have the answers and the solutions to my worry and fear through which I've created limitation, pain, and separation. I ask you for Your Wisdom, guidance, and understanding to get through this time of confusion. Please give me an extra vision to connect to infinite possibilities. I ask you for a higher consciousness. Fill me with your unconditional love. Thank you and I love you. Amen.

RECONNECTING WITH SPIRIT

Strengthening our relationship with the Divine can be the most rewarding experience of our life. Once you're open to it, your 1:1 guidance from God can catapult you into a new level of your most exciting reality you'd never even considered possible. On the other hand, it can also cause confusión, make you second guess yourself. In the beginning, you may ask yourself: *Was it really divine guidance? Or, I'm not getting anything, I`m not hearing anything. Why isn´t God revealing Himself to me?*

Let´s not go that way. Allow yourself to pause for a moment. Let`s set a different intention here. May our intention together be to reconnect with spirit in a way that will bring our souls and our lives back into balance to receive the confirmation that the answer does indeed come from a higher power. Deal? OK!

Faith is believing. Not questioning

I´m well aware that during your life, you might have had plenty of reasons to get angry with God. Things didn´t work out the way you planned. That man hurt your feelings, money failed you, a relative of yours suddenly died. In short, life was just too much to handle. Did you ask: *Why me? Why does it always have to be so hard on me, God?* Yet, no answer came from above.

Apparently, no one heard your prayers. You felt spiritually abandoned. Disappointed. Orphaned. I feel you. So, you may ask: *how am I suppose to establish a powerful relationship with God, after all this?* I can imagine it´s not easy. But I´m here to tell you it´s doable, or as Marie Forleo says, it´s ¨*figu-reable*¨.

Even though your judgments told you otherwise, God has never abandoned you — God has been preparing you for your greatest destiny. Trials, obstacles, and delays — those times tested your attitude. I can easily recall moments in my life where I too, was on my knees, literally. Yet, the one thing I promised myself during times of my deepest despair and depression was that no matter what happened, I would not use it to destroy my faith and turn my back on God. I made a decision to not blame God for any of my failures or become bitter by giving it a negative meaning. I knew I could change my circumstances by changing my feelings about them. My soul´s truth became this one:

God is with me through this. I trust He will guide me step by step back to bliss. This is not a punishment — it is just training. I`m becoming my most compassionate, beautiful and resourceful self through facing this obstacle — through this time of not knowing. With God, I can make it through this. At this moment surrender any thoughts of despair and helplessness. I choose again, and I choose love. I choose to smile, even through tears. Thank you, God, for this opportunity to grow my Soul.

With such an attitude, I immediately felt empowered and focused on the 3 things I COULD control: my thoughts, my emotions, and my attitude.

So let me ask you: Would you be willing to open your heart to God with me, despite all odds? If so, let me teach you…

SURRENDER INTO ALIGNMENT WITH GOD

> *The LORD is my shepherd; I shall not want.*
> *Even though I walk through the darkest valley*
> *I will fear no evil: for you are with me;*
> *— Psalm 23, Bible*

As divinely guided women we seek our wisdom, our resilience, and inner resourcefulness, through our spiritual practice of receiving divine guidance. We´re aware that our conditioned mind has a very limited perception of what´s truly possible for us. That´s why connection with spirit is our #1 priority. We gift ourselves the permission to receive the answers and the solutions we yearn for, not from our limited mind, but from the realm of the Infinite Possibilities.

A Queen lives her life to glorify God and elevate others. She lives her life in surrendered divine disposition. That is, her spiritual attitude shows a willingness to give away her life and her gifts to a cause bigger than herself, for the benefit of others. Her calling may at first make her slightly frightened, feel inadequate for such a task or simply doubt her abilities to bring it to fruition — yet through all these initial stages, she continues to willingly surrender herself to the calling God destined her for.

Feminine leadership is based on being led by the Spirit. Making space in our daily routines to hear from God. To use discernment and wisely follow through the guidance and assurance we receive from our higher self. Treat it like a gym for the soul. Your spiritual workout. Because God is there for you — but are you there for God? Instead of asking God to do things for you, begin asking: *Dear God, what can I do for you?*

Being both soft and strong is a combination that very few have mastered. We need to be capable of both to become a whole soul. While it may sound "masculine", becoming a fearless leader, it doesn't have to harden you as a woman. It can actually soften you, free you and bring out the best in yourself.

EMPOWERED FEMININE LEADERSHIP	OVERLY MASCULINE LEADERSHIP
Having it all	Doing all yourself
Thriving in community & Relationship	Isolating in self-sacrifice
Receiving spiritual guidance	The pressure to have all the answers
Abundantly supported by the universe	Stressed & Stretched
Living fully expressed as a woman	Compartmentalising your identity

A QUEEN SEEKS DIVINE GUIDANCE

When you pray, God listens. When you listen, God speaks. And when you believe, God is moving mountains for you.

God cares for us spiritually. Our soul is comprised of our mind, will, and emotions. There's not one person on the planet who hasn't experienced some kind of pain, disappointment or grief in their soul. But the good news is this: our Shepherd cares for us, and He is able to restore our souls to peace. He restores and heals our minds and emotions, renewing and strengthening our lives. Surrendering into alignment with God brings automatic ease without needing, forcing, pushing and trying too hard. You know you´re backed up by invincible forces. And that things can instantly change for you.

As a Queen, you must train yourself and co-create with God a state called *Holy Determination* —a state of incredible resilience, unbreakable faith and a deep level of self-assurance that NOTHING will distract from what´s ultimately meant for you. In such a frame of mind, you dare to see the WHOLE picture of the sacrifices you need to make in order to achieve your desires.

In life, we prefer to be selective and choose only the nice and sweet side of our desires. That´s a Princess Mentality. If we don't take ownership of the difficult and heavy issues — time, money and effort required, (not to mention the secondary consequences such as the possibility of rejection, criticism, public hate or negative comments) we will never be able to succeed.

In a state of *Holy Determination*, supported by divine guidance, you accept everything that manifesting your desires will mean.

The voice of Holy Determination sounds like:

- I´m going to keep pursuing what God put in my heart. I´m going to keep available to receive what He once promised deep within my soul. I can´t be passive and resentful.
- I´ve got that FIRE burning deep within me — the knowledge that it´s meant for me
- I won´t let circumstances distract from what´s truly meant for me

What are you Holy Determined for? Write your reflections and any 'aha' moments below:

3 WAYS TO DEEPEN YOUR RELATIONSHIP WITH GOD

You can ask God for help and guidance. Change begins with knowing and respecting who you are and what God has called you to do. He is eager to bless you and help you find happiness. At first, it may not feel easy to learn how to pray in faith and to recognise God's answers, but it is possible.

The best way to create a personal relationship with God is the same way that you come to know anyone better — through communication and gradually establishing trust.

1. **Speak to Him through Prayer** — ask Him for reassurance and love. I used to think I needed some elaborate words I was taught in the Church to be heard by God. That´s far from the Truth. Speak to God in your own words, with friendly reverence, just as if speaking to on

old loving and supportive friend. Tell it like it feels and how you would like it to be. Pray not only with words but also with feelings. Put your elevated feelings in your prayers. One more thing: remember that prayer without action is not prayer — it's a delusion. Once you surrendered your intention to God, make sure you do your own part too…Just saying!

2. **Read holy texts and divinely inspired messages —** Study God. Study the word of God through the Bible, divinely inspired books, teachings or sermons. The more you immerse yourself in this vibration, the more your heart and intuition will resonate with the beauty of its wisdom. You will be able to apply it to your own field and personal circumstances in a more profound manner.

3. **Create your sacred space for the Divine —** it can be either a physical or spiritual space within you where you contemplate and reconnect with the Divine. It can be some corner in your home where you put a candle or a sacred picture, a journalling entry where you begin by asking God for his wisdom or a quiet meditation time where you focus your awareness that you are One with God. This is the space where his loving energy surrounds and involves you – with access and connection to it at all times.

Sometimes the rest we seek does not come from sleep. Sometimes the rest we seek comes from chasing our dreams. Sometimes the rest we seek comes from trusting God that our blessing is right around the corner.

Last but not least, I want to leave you with a shortlist of the Queenly Royal Standards that will add and support your powerful connection with God. Mark or circle those that need to be given particular attention.

Queens Royal Standards:

- **Self- care** — Honouring the needs of your body and fully inhabiting it
- **Dignity** — Recognising yourself as a divine feminine and trusting your intuitive wisdom
- **Beautiful entourage** — Walking and living amongst beauty
- **Conscious language** — Speaking your truth in a respectful and self-empowering way
- **Strong self-respect** — never wanting or seeking external validation
- **Daily self- empowerment** — Having a personal routine that strengthens your confidence, self-belief, and clarity of purpose
- **Sacred isolation** — Creating time and space for you and God.

VISUALISE YOUR HIGHEST SELF AND START SHOWING UP AS HER

A LETTER FROM GOD TO YOU, DIVINE QUEEN…

Dear Daugther,

Do you know that you are beautiful? You are.
Do you know I love you just as you are? I do.
Mountains may be shaken and the hills may be moved but I will still love you!

It is Me who created you, I knitted you together in your mother´s womb and I know you better than anyone on Earth.
I know your problems and burdens because I bear them with you. Remember, I will never leave you nor forsake you. Even if your close ones leave you — I will receive you. I will keep you safe in my tent in the day of trouble and set you high upon a rock. I will not slumber but watch over you in every hour of your life, so you can always lie down and sleep in peace.

I am always close to you. I follow you like a shadow.
Come to Me with the burden you carry and I will give you rest. Cast all your anxiety on Me because I care for you.

Even though you walk through the darkest valley do not fear because I AM with you. You will go on your way in safety and your feet will not stumble.

I will give you power and strength. I will give you an undivided heart and put a new spirit within you because I have called you to the most perfect life. If you want, I will teach you what you cannot see — how to change your heart. I will show you the way of life I want you to follow. Then, you will have live life to the fullest. I will do it through you.

Reject every kind of evil as although you have the right to do anything not everything is beneficial.

Remain pure in heart and you will see Me. Be modest in your behaviour and do not concentrate only on your beauty for it comes from inside and is revealed from your heart. Be noble and your life will become a gift for others.

Develop goodness in you and then you will find the greatest gift. Protect it from those who do not deserve to see it. And remember that where your treasure is, there your heart will be also. Keep away from empty talk and gossip so that only words helpful for building others up are spoken. Always be trustworthy. May your diligence speak for you. Wear honesty as you would handsome clothing and I will hear your every prayer.

I AM the God of Love. My love lives in you. However, in order to love others, you must first love yourself. You are beautiful the way I have created you. You are like a lily amongst thorns. So do not compare yourself to others because your value does not lie in what others think of you.

Do not fear — there is no place for fear in love. Love your husband and you will not get lost or stumble. Be your husband´s crown through your nobleness and the one I have given to you will be amazed. You are his and he is you. Fight for your love and be faithful to him for it was out of my will that you have become one. Your beauty and joy will be his delight. Surrender to him because this is my will. I desire harmony between you and the man I have given to you. Therefore, forgive him whenever he hurts you. I know it is difficult but search for strength in Me.

I am your God. I can do everything — nothing is impossible for Me. It is enough for you to remain in Me and I will give you the desire of your heart. Now, precisely at this moment, I know what you need before you ask Me. Because I love you so much and care about you. I will never leave you.

Come to Me, my darling, my beautiful one.

There is only a question — who do you want to be? What do you want to choose? Do you want to transform your life?

I am waiting patiently for your response.

I love you,
God

Chapter Ten

QUEENS SURRENDER (ONLY) TO KINGS

*"I owe you a full man. The Little Boy won't be enough.
I owe you a full woman. The Little Girl bothers even myself. "*
— GERARD WALPER

You yearn for an intimate partner. A partner who matches your passion for life and is your equal in every way — someone who shares your values and vision to create a better world.

So often though, what we look for in a man are the parts we believe to be lacking within ourselves. The confidence, inner strength, material success, or creative expression. The Princess within us may desire a tall, handsome multimillionaire in a Ferrari, dressed in a Hugo Boss suit with a beautiful villa. Nothing wrong if he happens to be the one with such features… But let's be a Queen about it. Let's go much deeper. Let's take a look at what would really be a true service to the evolution of your soul. Is it really his possessions, status or looks?

The Queen within us craves more. She appreciates a man's presence, the clarity of his life purpose, his empowered masculine energy, feeling emotionally protected and safe around him. Someone spiritually developed and psychologically mature. A man with a strong bond to his father and with a similar, healthy relationship to the other men in his family. A man brave enough to take action to claim you. A man who has a love for life. A King of a man.

Ask your own soul: what is truly important to you in a partnership?

What are you looking for in a partner that you can develop in yourself?

HONOUR YOUR PAST LOVINGLY

"Spiritual practice is the capacity to offer your love even when you feel hurt, closed down, tense, angry, misunderstood, rejected, hated — and staying open in love, even in the most difficult circumstances"
— DAVID DEIDA, SPIRITUAL TEACHER

Before calling in your King, you will be asked to respect the past experiences of your heart. Every ex-partner was teaching you, in some way, how to love. Yes, he was your teacher of love. Underneath any secret resentment or sense of injustice done to you, there was always love. The healing of your heart consists of accessing that love, above our pride, ego, and sense of hurt.

The love between a man and a woman is sacred. It belongs only to them only. Please don't share your past experiences with a new partner, that's my honest advice. Keep it classy. Keep it to yourself. Sharing such details would only weaken your new relationship and moreover, by complaining about your ex, you are unconsciously asking for more of the same from your new man. So, never speak about your ex. Never speak badly about him out loud or in public. Show yourself to be respectful, regardless of any possible hurt from the past.

Many women, after a break-up, feel like they gave too much of their time and resources to a man and that their partner did not give equally in return. Deep within, they still want to punish him.

Please don't allow your children to become involved in any spiritual hurt towards your former partner or husband. Please don't involve your children in the matters of adults. Such behavior is below you, spiritually immature and definitely, not worthy of a Queen.

Also, please don't rush into another relationship too quickly. Allow your heart to grieve. To live out that love until you're done. Until your heart is open again.

HEALING EXERCISE:

Now, please recall an image of your ex-partner. Look at his face. Deep within your soul, you can direct these words to him:

(His name), thank you for everything you have given me.
Now I can see you gave me so much.
I am taking it with gratitude and I will keep it as a treasure.
What I have given you, I gave it willingly. Please keep it.
I hope it serves you well. You will always have a place in my heart
as my ex-partner or father of our children.
You participate in my successes and you too can enjoy them.

Notice your sensations. Notice what insights and feelings were coming to you while expressing the above words. You can journal about your "aha moments" from this exercise. You need to truly accept the relationship for what it was and seek closure from it.

WHY DO YOU KEEP ATTRACTING WEAK MEN?

Another aspect of the necessary feminine healing I saw among my clients is the "Too strong woman syndrome". Let me give you an example:

So there she is. A strong, resilient, resourceful and ambitious woman taking over the role of a man in a relationship. There HE is. Undecided, unsure, reserved, weak and without vital forces, forever "the little boy". So many women can recognise this image. And so do men.

There are various reasons behind such a dynamic:

- Missing fathers due to work commitments (either at home or being required to move away), stress at work, political conflicts, and wars
- Feminism as a karmic justice
- Social isolation and broken family bonds (the death of community and rise of individualism)

What made you feel exactly the same way in your childhood as you feel now when your man is weak and what are those feelings? Maybe impatience, loneliness, being unloved, resentment, anger, frustration, fear, disdain…Where are all these feelings leading you? What is that weak man, either from your past or in your present life guiding you towards?

Well, TOWARDS YOUR MUM. It's with her that you experienced all these emotions. Your man, probably unconsciously, yet lovingly, is guiding you towards your mother.

What can we do about it?

When you're going through emotional turmoil and pain related to the weakness you see and feel in that man, follow these steps:

1. Give yourself space and permission to feel those emotions. Breathe them. Say to that emotion: *You´re allowed to be here with me.*
2. Imagine that man in front of you.
3. Now, turn your head, look in a different direction and see your mum. In your mind's eye say to her:

It has to do with you, mum.
I felt all those emotions with you.
It´s in the relationship with you that I felt…(and say what did you feel)

4. Next, look at that man again and say to him:

It has nothing to do with you.
Thank you for guiding me towards my mum.
Underneath all this suffering, I can see how much you serve me and how much you love me.
Now, you can be masculine. You can be you.
I will resolve the issues I have.

IF YOU FOCUS ON THE HURT, YOU WILL CONTINUE TO SUFFER. IF YOU FOCUS ON THE LESSON, YOU WILL CONTINUE TO GROW.

FROM WOUNDED TO AN AWAKENED WOMAN

"The most beautiful love stories are written when two people have done the inner work and have laid down their ego nature to embrace unconditional love — a higher love that is selfless and grounded in the divine."
— DANIEL NIELSEN

In order to attract a King, you have to be empowered in your feminine Rich Soul. A woman confident in her femininity is a woman who, deep within her soul, is close to her mother — and spiritually connected and empowered by other women in her feminine lineage.

A man strong in his masculinity is a man who deep within stands close to his father — spiritually enlightened by other men in his lineage.

Often, the man in your life will reflect back to you the dynamics with your own mother. What hasn't been fully healed and processed within you, will be mirrored in the relationship with your partner.

Look at the table below and highlight those aspects that require more attention and work for your awakening. Reflect on which aspects need shifting and strengthening.

WOUNDED WOMAN	AWAKENED WOMAN
Afraid to speak her truth	Honours her truth
Lacks self-worth	Knows her worth
Tolerates toxic people	Sets loving boundaries
Seeks external validation	Feels validated from within
People pleases	Inspires others to shine
Apologises for who she is	Lives unapologetically
Has negative self-talk	Speaks gently to herself

WHAT IS A HEALTHY RELATIONSHIP ANYWAY?

A healthy relationship is one of two spiritually and emotionally mature adults. A relationship's dynamics won't work as long as you are playing the good mother to your man, or expect him to be a father figure to you. Such a dynamic is destined to fail sooner or later. Always. It's based on projections and not grounded in reality.

A meaningful relationship means you come together to make each other better. Believe in each other. Support each other. Build each other up. Be their peace, not their problem.

As many of us didn't receive a complete model of a healthy partnership when younger, we must deepen our understanding in this matter through books, seminars, and successful role models.

Janet Woititz, an American psychologist and researcher in her famous book "Struggle for Intimacy", presents the following 6 rules of a healthy relationship:

1. I can be me.
2. You can be you.
3. We can be us.
4. I can grow.
5. You can grow.
6. We can grow together.

Such a relationship does not interfere in the process of our being and becoming. We are free to be us. We are free to grow. We are free to keep taking responsibility for our own happiness.

What a contrast to what's commonly seen in our society: most relationships are based on co-dependency, disrespect, criticism and a forced pleasing of one another.

In the table below, you can compare the factors related to both wounded and awakened love, to gain more awareness around the healthy pillars of an awakened relationship.

WOUNDED LOVE	**AWAKENED LOVE**
Criticism	Acceptance
Insecure	Confident
Controlling	Surrendering to love
Lack of trust	Trust and respect
Co-dependent	Soul-dependent
Shuts down	Heart is open
Tries to change and fix	Understands and supports
Only physically attracted	Attracted beyond physical

IMPORTANT: Take responsibility for the necessary healing in your relationship. Remember that men deserve to be respected. To be told they're handsome, that their efforts and hard work are appreciated. How do you expect to be his

Queen if you treat him like a servant?

A QUEEN DOESN'T WANT ANYONE WHO DOESN`T WANT HER

The feminine within us yearns to be loved. As a result, we often love too much and become desperate for it to be reciprocated. Yet, no relationship is ever worth sacrificing your dignity or self-respect.

Never beg for love. Never beg someone to be with you. Never beg for attention, commitment, time and effort. Keep your instincts alert. Remember that the love of a man is expressed through his action. If a man isn't willing and strong enough to chase you and claim you, well, move on.

If you desire marriage and to be a wife, yet after years together no one has ever seen the engagement ring, get out of the delusion. Never commit to 'what might be'. If he isn't taking any action or effort to take you out or to spend time with your parents, please don't justify that. That's naive. Here comes a truth bomb: he simply doesn't care as much as you do and actions speak louder than words. Sorry to be this blunt, it runs in my Slavic blood!

You should never have to ask to feel wanted. Begging is demanding and degrading. If someone isn't willing to share with you these things, with their arms wide open — it's not worth it. Avoid relationships that separate you from yourself and your soul. Leave behind anything and anyone that divorces you from your truth.

#Queens Rule

STOP LETTING PEOPLE WHO DO SO LITTLE FOR YOU, CONTROL SO MUCH OF YOUR MIND, FEELINGS AND EMOTIONS

Know your worth. Know the difference between what you´re getting and what you deserve because, if you find yourself constantly trying to prove your worth to someone, you've forgotten your value.

So instead, make yourself available only to a full man. The actions of full men are clear, concrete and daring. Save yourself the time of hoping, wishing and praying. Say adiós to Little Boys.

THE LOVE OF A MAN TOWARDS A WOMAN IS EXPRESSED THROUGH ACTION.

THE LOVE OF A WOMAN TOWARDS A MAN IS EXPRESSED THROUGH RESPECT

WHO DOES THE QUEEN ATTRACT?

In terms of a relationship, she attracts Kings, men who are solid and grounded. Men who adore her strength equally with her deep feminine core and vulnerability. Men who have a strong masculine side and foundation. A King is a compliment to a life already well-lived.

Professionally, she attracts those who know that she is the one who will take them to the next level - people who admire her and recognise her leadership qualities.

WHO DOES THE QUEEN REPEL?

People who don't want to take responsibility for themselves, their life or their issues. Because she demands ownership, these people won't like that she holds them to also be accountable. She will repel men who are not strongly in tune with their masculinity and femininity.

HEALING YOUR CORE ESSENCE

Our fullest potential is found in balancing the divine feminine and divine masculine energies within ourselves. Both men and women carry feminine and masculine wisdom and traits. However, sometimes one or both of these energies are out of balance, silenced, wounded, misunderstood or disrespected. A balanced energy system is very important for healing.

Take a look at the table below and highlight those aspects of your life that need strengthening.

Notice: Are they on the feminine or masculine side of your energy?

DIVINE FEMININE	DIVINE MASCULINE
Intuition	Logic
Nurturing	Protective
Flow	Discipline
Non- linear	Linear
Love radiance	Consciousness
Surrender	Direction
Receiving	Giving

7 Ways to Strengthen Your Inner Masculine:

1. Examine your wound surrounding the masculine
2. Take self-responsibility.
3. Contact your inner father.
4. Find a masculine teacher or guide who you admire.
5. Connect with your inner warrior.
6. Be assertive and take no bullshit!
7. Stop being passive and start being active.

7 Ways to Embrace Your Divine Feminine:

1. Honour yourself as a woman — get in touch with your creative, nurturing, compassionate, intuitive self
2. Trust your intuition, your direct link to the divine
3. Allow yourself to be vulnerable in a safe space
4. Connect with your sisterhood and community
5. Bring the divine into your body - God is in every part of you and your senses. Make your body sacred, love and accept your body more, it is a blessing to enjoy
6. Connect with Mother Nature with your bare feet
7. Give attention to your 5 senses: taste, smell, touch, hearing, and sight

POWER COUPLE DYNAMICS

Kings and Queens are a team to themselves, together against the world.

It's a sublime and exclusive relationship. A divinely ordained sacred union. Nobody can come between a King and a Queen. No mum, no dad, no siblings or friends. They defend each other. They push each other and see themselves as teammates, not competition. They form a power couple while still maximising their individuality.

A Queen will never be too much" for a King. Kings are never intimidated by a Queen's power or strength. In fact, Kings are not intimated by anybody. He acknowledges his Queen's feminine power and her beauty. He rejoices in her light.

It is said that the quality of a man's wife is an indication of his own intelligence. On the other side, a man who doesn't protect, offends you and wants to empty your self-esteem is not a King. A true Queen is not available for any verbal denigration or physical abuse. Do it once and they will lose that Queen forever.

A true King also deserves his Queen's unapologetic respect. You cannot behave towards a King like he's a clown, because, like you, a King can only be disrespected ONCE – he holds your values and self-worth, so when a King decides to go away, he too doesn't return.

Remember, you are a team – both in thought and in the body. A team of equals.

IF YOU WANT TO CHANGE THE WORLD, LOVE A MAN

If you want to change the world love a man; really love him
Choose the one whose soul calls to yours clearly who sees
you; who is brave enough to be afraid.

Accept his hand and guide him gently to your hearts blood
Where he can feel your warmth upon him and rest there
And burn his heavy load in your fires.

Look into his eyes, look deep within and see what lies dor-
mant or awake or shy or expectant there
Look into his eyes and see there his fathers and grandfathers
and all the wars and madness their spirits fought in some
distant land, some distant time
Look upon their pains and struggles and torments and guilt;
without judgment
And let it all go
Feel into his ancestral burden
And know that what he seeks is a safe refuge in you
Let him melt in your steady gaze
And know that you need not mirror that rage
Because you have a womb, a sweet, deep gateway to wash
and renew old wounds

If you want to change the world love a man, really love him
Sit before him, in the full majesty of your woman in the breath of your vulnerability
In the play of your childhood innocence in the depths of your
death
Flowering invitation, softly yielding, allowing his power as
a man
To step forward towards you…and swim in the Earth's
womb, in silent knowing, together

And when he retreats…because he will…
flees in fear to his cave…

Gather your grandmothers around you,
envelope in their wisdoms
Hear their gentle shusshhhed whispers, calm your frightened girls' heart urging you to be still
and wait patiently for his return
Sit and sing by his door, a song of remembrance,
that he may be soothed, once more

If you want to change the world, love a man, really love him
Do not coax out his little boy
With guiles and wiles and seduction and trickery
Only to lure him…to a web of destruction
To a place of chaos and hatred
More terrible than any war fought by his brothers
This is not feminine, this is revenge
This is the poison of the twisted lines
Of the abuse of the ages, the rape of our world
And this gives no power to woman, it reduces her as she cuts
off his balls
And it kills us all

And whether his mother held him or could not
Show him the true mother now
Hold him and guide him in your grace and your depth
Smoldering in the center of the Earth's core
Do not punish him for his wounds that you think don't meet
your needs or criteria
Cry for him sweet rivers
Bleed it all back home

If you want to change the world love a man, really love him
Love him enough to be naked and free
Love him enough to open your body and soul to the cycle of
birth and of death
And thank him for the opportunity

As you dance together through the raging winds and silent woods
Be brave enough to be fragile and let him drink in the soft, heady petals of your being
Let him know he can hold you, stand up and protect you
Fall back into his arms and trust him to catch you
Even if you've been dropped a thousand times before
Teach him how to surrender by surrendering yourself
And merge into the sweet nothing, of this worlds' heart

If you want to change the world, love a man, really love him
Encourage him, feed him, allow him, hear him, hold him, heal him
And you, in turn, will be nourished and supported and pro-
tected
By strong arms and clear thoughts and focused arrows
Because he can, if you let him, be all that you dream

If you want to love a man,
love yourself, love your father, love your brother, your son, your ex-partner;
from the first boy you kissed, to the last one you wept over

Give thanks for the gifts; of your unraveling to this meeting
Of the one who stands before you now
And find in him the seed to all that's new and solar
A seed that you can feed to help direct the planting
To grow a new world, together.

by Lauren Wilce

YOUR FUTURE IS GOLD

The past can be beautiful. A memory. A dream…
But it's not a place to live. And NOW is the time.
The only way out…
is up.

Your time to be a Queen is NOW. Your time to leave the fear behind and, claim your greatness is NOW. Your time to live out your best life is NOW.

You are ready. You know enough. You've been through enough.

Return to this book anytime you need a confidence boost. Keep it close to you and gift it to your best friend. Not only you will expand your circle of Queens but you will also gain valuable support.

Your future is gold — an avalanche of abundant, divine blessings is flowing towards you now as you claim your Queenhood.

Remember to look your future success squarely in the eyes. Don't turn away. Remember that the price of success must be paid in advance. Remember to keep your dignity and a humble heart along the way.

Respect is the keyword that will open many doors for you.

Respect yourself fiercely and be respectful towards others.

Be bold.
Be daring.
Be unapologetically you.

THE WORLD NEEDS YOUR FEMININE MAGIC.

BEFORE YOU CLOSE THIS BOOK...

I'd like to present to you someone special.

Someone who gives all his Heart and Soul into raising global consciousness on our planet, for people like you and me.

Someone who is relentless in helping others transform their biggest challenges into their biggest blessings.

To my mentor
LAIN GARCIA CALVO

I'd like to dedicate a special mention here to my supportive mentor whom I had the honour of learning from and thanks to whom this book and my career as an author was made possible.

Thank you, Lain.

My gratitude to you is beyond words.
So is my respect for all that you teach, embody and share.
May God tenderly bless you always on your path.

THE BOOK OF MY BREAKTHROUGH

"The Voice of Your Soul"

THE DAY I RECEIVED THIS BOOK

I will never forget the day I received this book… 11 AM in the morning. I was still lying alone in bed in my apartment in London. Depressed. Demotivated. Bored. Helpless and hopeless.

All I could see through the window day after day was a grey, rainy sky. Suddenly, I heard a noise. The doorbell ringing. I didn't even feel like bothering to open the door to anyone. It rang again, and again…Something inside me told me I should move. It was a delivery man with my copy of *"The Voice of Your Soul"*!

I touched it. I innocently smiled at the title. I hugged this blue book to my Heart. I prayed it would be THE BOOK that would finally help me to get out of my helpless state I was in, my anxiety, despair and so much more.
I quickly ran upstairs and began to avidly read it. Immediately I felt uplifted. I stopped being that "miserable, depressed Justina" and knew that I would be over all the difficulties of the past months…
Each page lifted my Spirit.

It reminded me of that little voice within I used to follow... until I betrayed it and all my confusion and drama began.

The teaching inside the book challenged me to elevate myself and my thinking above my passive victim mentality. The Law of the Universe explained in it began to make sense and all the mistakes I had made out of ignorance. The soulful message began to give me some hope and inner motivation to overcome my circumstances. I desired to take my power back and this book finally taught me the "how" in a way I could easily understand and implement.
I began dreaming again. Dancing again. Loving myself again.

"The Voice of your Soul" rescued me from a miserable depression into being seen in all my glory and with a full expression of my soul.

Dear Soul Sister, I couldn't recommend it more to you. Give yourself this Soulful gift. Treat your Soul to Peace and Truth. Lain's book has completely reconnected me with my Soul and brought so many blessings into my life. I'm sure his teachings will bless your life too in countless ways.

HOW CAN I GET THE BOOK?

1. Visit either Amazon: *"The Voice of your Soul"* by Lain Garcia Calvo

2. Order it directly from Lain's website:
www.laingarciacalvo.com

ACKNOWLEDGMENTS

To my beloved mother, Marta — my best spiritual teacher; to my beloved father, Wieslaw, my best mentor — for giving me the gift of Life. I will do something great with it!
To the best sister in the entire world, Dominika and my whole family. I love you so much!
To Bart. My friend, I thank God for you every morning because your presence in my life is a blessing. Thank you for always being able to count on you. For your true friendship and being by my side through thick and thin. You are my brother from another mother.
To Monika Kowalska, thank you for understanding my Soul. For the countless talks we have had, for the hours you've spent listening to me, advising me and supporting my spiritual growth. Thank you for the books you have recommended and all the teas you have made for me in the last 14 years.
To Luis Delgado Conde — for teaching me not only Spanish, but also having the courage to believe in my dreams regardless of distance, money, and obstacles.
To Thomas Gerer — for your wisdom, for believing in me more than I have ever believed. For opening my eyes and teaching me a new world of possibilities.
To Gina DeVee, for being an example of a Divine Woman and showing me what a life without limits means according to our dreams.

To Nancy Florence, for demonstrating so much, for that night when you told me *"Justina, keep the faith."* This faith has saved me. Your friendship is my treasure.
To Vítor, for your generosity, our laughter and jokes together, for always taking such tender care of me. You're special and I thank God for all that I've been able to learn with you.

To all my private clients for trusting me and inviting me into their worlds. Being able to serve you has always been an honour and a pleasure. I remain at the service of your life and your Soul.
And last but not least, to my beloved grandmother Sofia — my guardian angel.